"As a leading voice for reformation in the twenty-first century, Mark Dever calls evangelicals to love the church as much as we love Jesus. In this exposition of 1 Corinthians he gives clear pastoral guidance for the difficult problems addressed in a difficult book of the Bible, confronting not only the controversial issues that always face the church, but also the spiritual dangers that lurk behind them."

—Philip Graham Ryken, Senior Minister,
Tenth Presbyterian Church, Philadelphia, Pennsylvania

"*Twelve Challenges Churches Face* is a careful exposition of 1 Corinthians. It is both theological and practical in its goal to foster healthy churches. You will be edified and encouraged by Pastor Dever's treatment of important issues that confront the church on a daily basis."

—Daniel L. Akin, President, Southeastern Baptist Theological Seminary,
Wake Forest, North Carolina

"Few books of the Bible are as relevant to the modern church as 1 Corinthians, and few pastors are building their churches as faithfully as Mark Dever. In *Twelve Challenges Churches Face*, Mark takes Paul's counsel to the Corinthians and applies it to churches today with compelling clarity and wisdom. Pastors, churches, and individuals will all be—just like the Corinthians—instructed, corrected, encouraged, and pointed to the Savior."

—C. J. Mahaney, Sovereign Grace Ministries

Crossway books by Mark Dever:

The Message of the Old Testament: Promises Made
The Message of the New Testament: Promises Kept
Nine Marks of a Healthy Church
The Deliberate Church: Building Your Ministry on the Gospel (co-author)
The Gospel and Personal Evangelism
In My Place Condemned He Stood: Celebrating the Glory of the Atonement
  (co-author)

TWELVE
CHALLENGES
CHURCHES
FACE

MARK DEVER

CROSSWAY BOOKS

WHEATON, ILLINOIS

Cover design: Jon McGrath
Cover photo: iStock
First printing 2008
Printed in the United States of America

Unless otherwise indicated, Scripture quotations are from *The Holy Bible: New International Version.*® Copyright © 1973, 1978, 1984 by International Bible Society. Used by permission of Zondervan Publishing House. All rights reserved.

    The "NIV" and "New International Version" trademarks are registered in the United States Patent and Trademark Office by International Bible Society. Use of either trademark requires the permission of International Bible Society.

Scripture quotations marked ESV are from *The Holy Bible, English Standard Version*® copyright © 2001 by Crossway Bibles, a publishing ministry of Good News Publishers. Used by permission. All rights reserved.

Scripture quotations marked KJV are from the *King James Version* of the Bible.

Library of Congress Cataloging-in-Publication Data
Dever, Mark.
    12 challenges churches face / Mark E. Dever.
        p. cm.
    Includes index.
    ISBN 978-1-58134-944-3 (hc)
    1. Bible. N.T. Corinthians, 1st—Criticism, interpretation, etc. 2. Church.
  3. Sin—Christianity. I. Title. II. Title: Twelve challenges churches face.

    BS2675.6.C5.D48 2008
    262—dc22

                                         2007044622

LB	16	15	14	13	12	11	10	09	08
	9	8	7	6	5	4	3	2	1

To Michael and Adrienne Lawrence,
dear friends for more than twenty years,
and sweet partners in the gospel who,
like the household of Stephanas,
"have devoted themselves to the service of the saints" (1 Cor. 16:15).

CONTENTS

PREFACE

TWELVE CHALLENGES CHURCHES FACE

Do you think the biggest problems facing your church are extraordinary situations, providing better grief counseling, or improving your singing? I think God's Word has some other ideas of what challenges your church faces. Some more ordinary challenges. Some more theological challenges.

I've never bought into the idea that theology is always academic, obscure, and secondary. To me, knowledge of God has always drawn me to know God (hardly an obscure or merely academic task!). The Bible presents example after example of theology applied to life. And one of the prime examples of this is 1 Corinthians.

First Corinthians is a fascinating book. It's a confusing book. It's a book that is mined for proof texts on various topics. And it is undeniably a powerful book. Paul had clearly discovered in Christ the freedom to lay aside his own rights in order to love and serve others. This work of Christ's Spirit in him brought insights into the nature of preaching the gospel, of living a holy life as a whole church, the willingness to be wronged, to forgo rightful pleasure if other people would benefit from his abstinence. On and on we could go. The love Paul knew from Christ was used by the Holy Spirit to unlock the riches of both understanding and applying the gospel to the life of a congregation that Paul knew and loved.

In this letter, 1 Corinthians, Paul astonishes the pastor (at least, he did me). When he was facing the most normal of problems (division in the church, worldliness, selfishness, and others) he reached for deeply theological responses. Paul called the Corinthian congregation to be not divided but united, not worldly but holy, not selfish but loving. That's not the surprising part. The surprising part is how he argued this with them. He called them to forsake divisions, because God is one. He called them to forsake sin, because God is holy. He called them to forsake selfishness, because God is loving. In all of this, the governing presupposition is not that the church should operate by a rule book of spiritual manners and etiquette, but that the church is a living reflection of the living God. There is one God. He is holy and has given himself in love. His church, therefore, should reflect his own character; we should be united and holy and loving or else we lie about him! That is a powerful thought.

I hope and pray that these sermons will provoke for you encouraging meditation on God, on how he has loved us in Jesus Christ, and on how that should provoke us to seek to live in that same love.

Thanks to Crossway for initiating and pursuing this project, and special thanks to Lydia Brownback—capable, kind, and patient editor.

These are a series of sermons I preached at the Capitol Hill Baptist Church in Washington DC from the end of August 2005 until the beginning of January 2006, which explains the New Year's introduction to the final chapter and also the opening illustration of chapter 11, "Death," which was the title of my sermon on Christmas morning 2005. The sermons were used of God in my life, in our congregation's life, and I pray that they will be used in your own life, and even in the life of your congregation.

Mark Dever, Washington DC
January 2008

1

FORGETFULNESS

1 CORINTHIANS 1:1–9

Young people today think of Moby not as the first name of a whale, but as a multi-platinum-selling recording artist. He released his first album twenty-two years ago as a teenager and member of the band *The Vatican Commandos*. His best-selling album is his 1999 release called *Play*, which has sold over ten million copies so far. Born Richard Melville Hall in 1965 in Manhattan, he has always been known simply as Moby. He is a direct descendant of Herman Melville, the well-known author, whose most famous work was *Moby Dick*. Moby has achieved a great deal of success, and although most young people know Moby's connection to the author, many don't know that Moby is a self-confessed Christian. He says he became a Christian when he was about twenty years old, when a friend encouraged him to read the Gospels. He read them, and that's when, as Moby recounts it, he was converted.

I read an article about Moby provocatively titled, "The Two Sides of Moby: Why He Loves Jesus but Not the Church."[1] While that's not quite what Moby is quoted as saying in the article, the sentiment is common enough—and understandable enough. Jesus is a figure of intense interest and even admiration for millions. His stories and sayings still inhabit our minds two thousand years after he taught on the other side of the globe. He published no books, founded no dynasty, led no army, and governed no nation, but his images and stories and teachings and followers have girdled the globe, presenting a message of a Savior who sacrifices himself out of love. And to most, this is *compellingly beautiful.*

Then there is the church. If you have grown up in a church, you have reasons to be disillusioned. The church seems like a boring topic for most and a duty reluctantly fulfilled for many. In stark contrast with many of the unforgettable sayings of Christ, we can't remember what we heard in most sermons ten minutes after we get home. People around the world aren't interested in our church; for that matter, people just around the corner aren't either! Churches have published books and fielded armies and ruled kings and even so, if you introduce the topic of the church, you'll often find it met with responses ranging from a mild disinterest to a real dislike.

We can understand why. Churches say they have the best and most important news in the world—they have the answer to our problems, they are God's embassies on earth—yet churches are made up of people like you and me, people who are grumpy, irritable, unfaithful, and selfish. We become too possessive of small things and too casual about great ones. We become too defensive for ourselves and ignore God. We talk of love, but we too often give ourselves over to hate—even in church.

In this book we are going to think about this topic of the church and her challenges, using Paul's first letter to the Corinthians as our framework. The epistle has a number of passages that are well known, such as chapter 13, the "love chapter," and chapter 15 about the resurrection. In working through this letter, we will be led into important passages on gender issues, spiritual gifts, lawsuits, and church discipline. Much of the letter is taken up with Paul addressing situations specific to the church in Corinth and answering questions put to him by some of the believers there.

God had used Paul to establish the church in Corinth during what we call his second missionary journey, which was also his first trip to Europe. Paul spent a year and a half there (likely in A.D. 50–51), working as a tentmaker or leather worker and preaching the good news about Jesus Christ. It was probably sometime a few years later during his two and a half years in Ephesus (between A.D. 52 and 55) that Paul wrote this letter.

Corinth was a major crossroads between the east and the west, between the southern portion of Greece and Athens and the northern parts of Greece. Ancient Corinth had been destroyed by the Romans in 146 B.C. A century later, in 29 B.C., Julius Caesar re-founded Corinth as a Roman colony. As a great trading center with mobile populations, it retained a reputation for immorality. Religions from all over the empire flourished in Corinth along with the newly resettled populations.

The church Paul had established in Corinth was young, full of life, and just as full of problems. No other church in the New Testament had more problems nor such a variety, and at the time of Paul's epistle, it was threatened with destruction. Leadership was misunderstood, people were self-deceived, the church was ridden with partisanship, pride, pretentiousness, and immorality. False teachers, super-spirituality, asceticism, and loveless selfishness were rife—not unlike some churches today, not unlike some of the churches that Moby has run into, and not unlike some churches you may have run into.

So how can we learn from Paul's epistle to this troubled church? We want to start where Paul started:

> Paul, called to be an apostle of Christ Jesus by the will of God, and our brother Sosthenes, To the church of God in Corinth, to those sanctified in Christ Jesus and called to be holy, together with all those everywhere who call on the name of our Lord Jesus Christ—their Lord and ours: Grace and peace to you from God our Father and the Lord Jesus Christ. I always thank God for you because of his grace given you in Christ Jesus. For in him you have been enriched in every way—in all your speaking and in all your knowledge—because our testimony about Christ was confirmed in you. Therefore you do not lack any spiritual gift as you eagerly wait for our Lord Jesus Christ to be revealed. He will keep you strong to the end, so that you will be blameless on the day of our Lord Jesus Christ. God, who has called you into fellowship with his Son Jesus Christ our Lord, is faithful. (1 Corinthians 1:1–9)

In our consideration of these verses, I hope you will be encouraged to meditate on some of the good things that God has done in the life of every Christian and in our churches. I want to ask four questions that I hope will prove fruitful as we follow Paul's instructions, inspired by God's Holy Spirit, for the Corinthian Christians and for us, too.

Remember Your Blessings

The first question to consider is this: have you forgotten your blessings? The Corinthian Christians were famous for their faults, and Paul is going to deal with these clearly and at some length later in the letter. First, however, he

focuses on something positive—the work of God's grace. Had the Corinthian believers received any blessings from God that Paul could point out?
Paul usually began his letters with a form of thanksgiving, but if there was a
church where he might not be able to do this, the church at Corinth would
be it. With all of the problems evident there, Paul had just reason to skip his
traditional opening, but he did not. When we need to speak critically about
a church—ours or another—how often do we pause and first consider the
evidences of God's work there?

The first evidence of God's work among the Corinthians is the fact
that Paul himself was writing to them (v. 2). Christ's apostle who had first
preached the gospel to them was now writing to them. Christian, we too
have God's Word—the Bible. We don't worship a picture or a statue or an
idea. We worship a personal God who speaks and has spoken to us. Like
these Corinthians, we are blessed people.

In fact, these Corinthians were *the church of God* as we see here in verse
2. Paul may have been the human instrument that founded this church,
but he acknowledges—for their sakes and his—that its members belong to
God. God looked at them, and he said, "These belong to me; they are mine.
They are *of me*. I have a special concern and care for them, a special regard
to their welfare." And the same is true of us, friends. Whatever challenges
we face in our churches, we are a church not owned by ourselves or by the
pastor; we are the church of God. The church—our church—is his creation,
his concern. Surely that reminds us of the importance of being in a church,
not merely that we should attend one, but that we are part of a choice and
privileged company. How great a blessing this is to us, to be a part of those
people who are God's special concern.

In verse 2 we also see the Corinthians described as those *sanctified in Christ
Jesus*. Paul brings this to the forefront before he gets to other matters. They
had been sanctified in Christ Jesus, declared and made holy in him. Grasping
the reality of sanctification is crucial to putting things in perspective. God
separates people from the world by putting them in Christ Jesus. We are
declared to be holy and righteous because Christ's holiness and righteousness
are accounted to us. Friends, if you are Christians, you do not need to labor
under condemnation. To do so is to ignore what God has done for you in
Christ. Christians are sanctified in Christ Jesus, and in him they are being
changed in their attitudes and actions, their loves and longings, to be more
like him. This is true of you, my friends, if you are Christians.

We read in verse 2 that Christians are *called to be holy*. We are called to
live lives that more fully reflect God's character. Holiness is our responsi-

bility and our destiny. It is God's work in us, work to which we are called as co-laborers. What a blessing that is! Rather than being lost in sin—today and for eternity—we are called to be holy.

We see in verse 3 that Paul prayed for *grace and peace* for the Corinthians. This standard greeting was used by Paul here as a deeply Christian prayer for God's mercy and for wholeness and soundness, especially concerning the believers' walk with God. These things are the reality of a Christian's life, aren't they? For the Corinthians and for us, the Christian life is marked by God's grace and by peace with him. Whatever challenges we may face in our congregations, we realize that Christ died to save us, and in so doing he bore our penalty. As a result, God's wrath is turned from us and his favor has been poured out on us. So great are our blessings that we can almost say that the things over which we struggle and suffer pain are small in comparison.

I remember reading about the last days of the Puritan minister William Gouge. Those days were marked by physical pain, as death normally is. But Gouge had always had a firm grip upon the gospel. He wrote once, "When I look upon myself, I see nothing but emptiness and weakness; but when I look upon Christ, I see nothing but fulness and sufficiency."[2] As he became more aged, he became more infirm in body, but his faith was strong. Friends remembered: "When he could scarcely hold the cup at the sacrament of the Lord's Supper, with his paralytic hand, while he carried it to his mouth; with a firm and fixed confidence he took hold of Christ, and with an holy and spiritual thirst, applied his blood to his soul."[3] Toward the end of Gouge's life, one friend wrote of him:

> In the most violent paroxysms, he said, "Well, yet in all these there is nothing of hell, or of God's wrath." His sufferings were never so deep, but he could see the bottom of them, and say, "Soul, be silent: soul, be patient. It is thy God and Father who thus ordereth thy condition. Thou art his clay, and he may tread and trample on thee as he pleaseth. Thou hast deserved much more. It is enough that thou art kept out of hell. Though thy pain be grievous, yet it is tolerable. Thy God affords some intermissions. He will turn it to thy good, and at length put an end to all: None of which things can be expected in hell." His afflictions greatly contributed to the exercise of his grace.[4]

We see in 1 Corinthians 1:4 that *Paul thanks God for the Corinthians*. If we were thinking in a secular way, the last thing in the world we could imagine is thanking God for them. The church had been full of problems ever since its founding, and as we go on in the letter we will see that there appeared to be some dissatisfaction in the church with Paul. Clearly a number of people did not think much of him. Paul's influence was being diminished so that he was seen as merely one of several competing "parties" within the church. Some were saying of his teaching, "Well, that's just *Paul's* opinion!" But regardless of that, what does Paul do? He thanks God for them. Friends, all true Christians are grounds for thanksgiving. God's work in each Christian, and in each congregation of Christians, is grounds for thanksgiving, a triumph of his mercy over sin, a testimony of his grace never to be forgotten.

Here in verse 4 Paul also expands on the grace he has mentioned already. He reminds the Corinthians that they have received God's grace *in Christ Jesus*. Whatever challenges Christians face, then and now, we know ourselves to be recipients of God's amazing grace; but we still need to remind ourselves of it.

Then, in verse 5, Paul tells the Corinthians that they had *been enriched in Christ in every way*. He reminds them that they are not spiritually impoverished but have been made better and given wonderful treasures. That is true of today's Christians, as well. Paul shows the breadth of this in the phrase "in every way." The Corinthians had been enriched in all their speaking. In Christ, their words could be used to speak the truth about God and to build each other up.

Paul also reminds the Corinthians that they had been enriched in all their knowledge. Corinth was a place that valued status, and knowledge was considered to be a way to status. So Paul used that fact to appeal to the basis of their richest knowledge, that which they had received in Christ. In Christ they had come to find the purpose of their lives, the reason for their existence, and the way they could be forgiven of their sins and come to know God. What better knowledge is there? Whatever these Christians may have been struggling with, whatever questions they had outstanding, whatever uncertainties or errors, they had been enriched in Christ in every way by the gospel in all their speaking and knowledge.

So have we, if we are Christians. We do not have to squander our words, uttering things that are unloving and untrue, words that are pointless or useless. The most important problems in the universe, and in our own lives, have been solved for us through the gospel. Do you think of yourself as having been enriched in every way? You have been in Christ. What peace or comfort can anyone lack who is in covenant with the Father of mercies?

But there is more still. We see in verse 6 that the testimony about Christ was confirmed in them. The Corinthians had become evidence of the truth of Paul's message. The Christian is living proof of the gospel. This church had become convinced of and had begun to experience and then to display the reality of the gospel of Jesus Christ. What a privilege this was for them and for us, too. Our lives reflect the truth of the message about Christ. We become filled with his image rather than our own, and in so doing our lives confirm gospel claims. Again, what a privilege to be so used by God in such a great task.

In fact, the Corinthians had been so enriched by Christ that Paul says in verse 7 that they didn't lack any spiritual gift. They lacked nothing that God could give them. We have all that we need for what God has called us to. As Christians we lack nothing we need to be built up in the Lord that he has not and will not supply. This is astounding. If you are anything like me, you are probably prone to think that you could do this or that if only you had this gift or that circumstance. But what we find here is that there is no spiritual gift that we lack as Christians. Since God has given us his only Son, how will he not with him give us everything that we need for life and godliness?

The Corinthian Christians, for all their problems, had an eager expectancy about them for the right thing. Paul comments on the fact that they eagerly wait for the revelation of Christ (v. 7). They had been given a sense of anticipation and, unlike our world's cruel counterfeits, this was an anticipation that would be met. Christians, here is yet another gift God has given you. How many times have you known disappointment when some cherished hope has been dashed, some eagerly anticipated moment taken from you? No matter! As Christians, we have been given an ultimate hope that will surely come to pass. This is a gift—a great gift.

In verse 8 there is a wonderful promise: believers will be kept strong to the end by Christ. These Corinthian Christians could be sure of divine strengthening to keep them going till the battle is won, till the race is over, till the job is done, till they have made it home. That is true for us, too, friends. If we are Christians, we have been given this great gift; we will persevere. I imagine that you sometimes feel weak. You wonder what is going to happen. Here we see an encouragement to realize that your well-being is in hands better and more powerful than your own.

Paul also reminds them that they would be blameless on the day of Christ (v. 8). When we read this letter, we find that the Corinthian church was full of people who were involved in various kinds of sin. But Paul assured them that "on the day of Christ" there will be nothing to lay against the Christian. We will be blameless. Not "merely" blameless, as one paraphrase puts it, not simply without "a guilty feeling"; we will not be reckoned guilty at all. There is something worse than feelings of self-condemnation, and that is condemnation by Almighty God. Guilt before God is real, and it is this guilt that Christians will be without on that final day of judgment.

Paul sums up their blessings in verse 9, telling the Corinthians that they had been called by God into fellowship with Christ. This is the state of a Christian. Where we once were at enmity with God, we have now been brought into a relationship with Christ. We have been and are being formed into a community with Christ. In giving us Christ, God has given us the best he could. As Paul later writes to the Christians in Rome, "He who did not spare his own Son, but gave him up for us all—how will he not also, along with him, graciously give us all things?" (Rom. 8:32).

Have you forgotten your blessings? Remember the blessings God has given you. There is a reason that Christians have sometimes been called simply "the blessed."

Who Has Blessed You?

The second question to consider as you meditate on this opening passage in 1 Corinthians is, have you forgotten who has blessed you? We must remember who has blessed us! We are helped by this person and that one. Someone gives us a gift. Another encourages us. Our birthdays are celebrated by family and friends. But in this passage we are reminded that the one who blesses us is God. It was God who willed Paul to be an apostle (v. 1) in the first place. So for us, friends, all the blessings enumerated in this chapter have come to us through God. We have this letter of Paul, and indeed all the Bible, only because of God. Behind all the blessings the Corinthians had been given through Paul was God. Paul was a conduit of these great blessings to the Corinthians, but it was God who had turned Paul from his sins, God who had called him to be an apostle, and God who had sent Paul to Europe.

Who were the apostles? They were those who through God's revelation and inspiration were authorized to speak for, to testify about, and to interpret the truth about God, and especially about Jesus Christ his Son. The apostles' authority—given by Christ himself—was final. We cannot appeal to some other authority and still call ourselves followers of Jesus Christ, because God has made his will known through the apostles. The apostles were given to the church by God.

Likewise, it is God who owns the assembly in Corinth (v. 2). The church belonged to God. The church was the creation of God and was owned by him. It was not Paul's church. It was God's. So Paul recognized in the

Corinthians—troubled as they were—that they were the special possession of God. God has become their father, as we see in verse 3, and he dispenses grace and peace. Grace and peace come from God, our Father. The blessing is from him and draws our minds back to him.

Paul, of course, recognizes that all of these blessings stand as tokens of God's love. So it is God who is always thanked by Paul (v. 4). He knows that God is the source of all these blessings. There is nothing good that Paul sees in the Corinthians that is not justly attributed to God himself. There is no spread of the gospel or growth of the church in Corinth that does not immediately draw Paul's mind back to God. When we read about the establishment of the church in Corinth (Acts 18), we find that Paul was discouraged and apparently preparing to leave it behind. But then we read in Acts 18:9–10, "One night the Lord spoke to Paul in a vision: 'Do not be afraid; keep on speaking, do not be silent. For I am with you, and no one is going to attack and harm you, because I have many people in this city.'" Paul knew that God was behind calling and blessing these people.

The grace that was given to the Corinthians in Christ Jesus (v. 4) was from God. It wasn't Paul against whom the Corinthians had sinned. It wasn't Paul who needed to extend grace to them. It was God against whom the Corinthians had sinned. If anyone's grace was needed, it was God's, and it was God's grace they received. The gospel holds out *God's* grace! Surely we understand that of our own lives as well. We thank God, because God is the source of our blessings.

We also see here that God is faithful (v. 9). God is not only our Creator and Father and gracious and peaceful—as if those blessings were not enough. God is also faithful. In the Greek language that Paul used, the wording more clearly reads "faithful is God," as if to stress the point. Paul considers this faithfulness particularly in connection with God's having called the Corinthians into fellowship with his Son, Jesus Christ. This great call—like Paul's own—had come from God. God was the one blessing and calling the Corinthians, and every blessing was to turn their minds and hearts back to him in thanksgiving and humility and joy and confidence. They were to remember that they were blessed and that God was the source of the blessings.

It is the same with Christians today. Our faith traces back from our blessings to the giver of them. All of the blessings we have been considering—wonderful though they are—draw our attention to the One who gives them, and so we praise God and thank him for his goodness. So our confidence is placed in him, our trust in him is excited, our reliance on him encouraged.

Have you forgotten *who* has blessed you? Remember who has blessed you—it is God! Remember that, my forgetful friends, and see what implications remembering might have for you today.

How Has God Blessed You?

The third question is this: have you forgotten how God has blessed you? God gave some of his blessings to the Corinthians through creation. Other blessings he gave through the ministry of Paul and other preachers among them, but throughout these verses Paul constantly points the Corinthians to the one through whom they had been supremely blessed—Jesus Christ.

It was the risen Christ who appeared to Paul and called him as an apostle (v. 1). The risen Christ appeared to Paul on the road to Damascus (Acts 9) and called him to himself and to be his apostle, and it was in Christ that the Corinthians had been sanctified (v. 2). Christ by his work declared the Corinthians holy, and he made them so.

In fact, again and again in this passage Jesus is called Lord (see vv. 2–3, 7–9). That Jesus Christ is Lord is the most widespread confession in these early verses of the letter. He is prayed to (v. 2). Consider that: Jesus Christ is legitimately prayed to. Most especially, Jesus Christ is the means of God's grace to the Corinthians (v. 4). How could a holy and righteous God love sinners? The answer is found in Jesus Christ. He is the one who, by his perfect life and substitutionary death, has merited and supplied God's grace to Christians. That is why we read that in him—in Christ—the Corinthians were enriched in every way (v. 5). It is only in and through Jesus Christ that Christians receive all God's blessings. Outside of Christ, God is our fearsome judge. He pursues us in his righteous claims over us. But our reconciliation to him, the great good news, comes only through Christ.

This is why Paul says in verse 6 that Jesus Christ was the one testified about to them. Who else would Paul tell them about? In what other name could Paul hold out to them such hope? Jesus Christ was the center of Paul's preaching, echoing what Peter once asked Jesus, "Lord, to whom shall we go? You have the words of eternal life. We believe and know that you are the Holy One of God" (John 6:68–69).

So it is Jesus Christ whose revelation is eagerly awaited (v. 7). The Christian hope for the future is focused on Jesus Christ and upon his return. It is Jesus Christ who would keep the Corinthians strong to the end (v. 8). It is Christ who perseveres with believers and causes them to persevere with him till death. The final day is referred to as *his* day (v. 8). That's because Christ is our final judge. It is in Christ that we are accepted. Whenever we celebrate the Lord's Supper, we are holding a dress rehearsal of that final day. It is into fellowship with Christ that we have been called into fellowship by God (v. 9). Richard Sibbes said:

> We may know our trust in the name of the Lord,
> being now conceived as a gracious Father in Christ,
> clothed with the relation of a father:
> for so we must trust him,
> not God absolutely,
> for there is no comfort in an absolute God,
> distinct from his relations;
> but when we apprehend him in relation as a sweet Father in Christ,
> in that name,
> then the nature of God is lovely to us,
> between whom and us there was an infinite distance before.
> Now Christ being Immanuel, God with us, has brought God and us
>   together.[5]

Our sharing in Christ is God's fundamental blessing to Christians.

We must not fail to notice how Paul refers to Jesus in verse 9—as God's Son. Many of us know the famous first question and answer of the Westminster Shorter catechism: "What is the chief end of man? Man's chief end is to glorify God and enjoy him forever." But nearly a century before the Westminster Assembly produced their famous catechism, the German reformer Ursinus produced the Heidelberg Catechism (1563) with an initial question and answer no less worthy of being known:

Question: What is your only comfort in life and in death?

> Answer: That I am not my own, but belong—body and soul—in life and in death—to my faithful Savior, Jesus Christ. He has fully paid for all my sins with his precious blood, and has set me free from the tyranny of the devil. He also watches over me in such a way that not a hair can fall from my head without the will of my Father in heaven; in fact, all things must work together for my salvation. Because I belong to him, Christ, by his Holy Spirit, assures me of eternal life and

makes me whole-heartedly willing and ready from now on to live for him.

Oh, my brothers and sisters, have you forgotten *how* God has blessed you? Remember how God has blessed you! He has blessed you—through Jesus Christ.

Have Others Forgotten Their Blessings?

The fourth and final question is this: have Christians around you forgotten their blessings? We must help other Christians remember the blessings of God. Consider the ministry of Paul. Certainly he was called to be an apostle of Jesus Christ by the will of God (v. 1). Paul had a unique ministry, and he expresses this fact to the Christians to whom he writes. He uses his apostolic title at the beginning of 1 and 2 Corinthians, Ephesians, Colossians, and 2 Timothy. Paul had been set apart by Christ to preach the gospel through-out the whole world. But in these letters Paul was concerned not simply to plant the gospel among them but also to help them with various issues in the church. He wrote to them to instruct and correct them, but we must not overlook the fact that Paul first identified the evident marks of God's grace among them. Primarily, Paul wrote to these believers in order to help them remember God's blessings in their lives and to help them work out the implications of them.

As we see in verse 2, Paul calls on the name of our Lord Jesus Christ. This is what marks out Christians—recognizing Christ as God and praying to him. Even apostles needed a savior. This was the man called Saul who had approved of the death of the first Christian martyr and had been active in imprisoning many other Christians. What an unlikely convert he was! But because of his past, he was a walking encouragement to other Christians, even before he said a word.

Do you see yourself as an unlikely convert? Paul was an unlikely convert, and when he was in Corinth, he saw some converts we might think unlikely. We read in Acts 18:8, "Crispus, the synagogue ruler, and his entire house-hold believed in the Lord; and many of the Corinthians who heard him believed and were baptized." When a frustrated mob was unable to get Paul successfully convicted and dealt with by Roman officials, "they all turned on Sosthenes the synagogue ruler and beat him in front of the court" (Acts 18:17). Crispus's successor in overseeing the synagogue, Sosthenes, became the focus of their frustrated anger. Whatever happened to him? "Paul . . . and our brother Sosthenes" (1 Cor. 1:1). It appears that he, too, was converted. Two consecutive synagogue rulers were converted in Corinth.

David Prior tells of what he calls "a parallel situation . . . at Oxford University in the early 1960s during the heyday of the Humanist Society. Its president was converted to Christ, which led to an extraordinary general meeting of the Society. The person then elected was himself converted within a few weeks, thus necessitating another extraordinary general meeting."[6] My friend, how impossible is it for you to consider calling on the name of our Lord Jesus Christ?

As remarkable as any of this, a nice summation of it all is found in verse 4. Paul thanks God for the Corinthians. What is the first thing that Paul said he did for these confused Christians? Did he say that he regretted ever making their acquaintance, or question their salvation, or warn others about them? He said none of these things. He thanked God for them. He understood that all of their particular sins and struggles were simply rearguard actions of the evil one in retreat. Important as some of these sins were—vivid in their ignorance, even more vivid in their defiance—they paled before God's saving grace in their lives. And so Paul begins with these people whom he must correct carefully and at points passionately by putting it all in perspective and thanking God for them, and even telling them that he was thanking God for them.

It is always wise to begin by noticing evidences of God's work in someone you must correct, even if there are other issues looming larger in your mind. Pausing to remind another, and yourself, of God's grace will make it easier for the erring one to hear the corrective words that you want to say, and it will also help you to have a more accurate perspective as you begin to discuss the need for correction. If you cannot see the evidences of God's grace in the one who needs correction, you may have a log in your eye, in which case maybe you should wait to speak about the other's speck until you can see the evidences of God's work in your brother or sister. My friends, if the one in error is a believer, God has purchased him or her, and his Spirit is at work there. If you cannot see that, you are failing to see the most important thing about that person.

We are not called to the same apostolic ministry as Paul was. But we can work to help others around us to notice and remember evidences of God's grace in their lives. Doing so will make us more loving and careful and observant and joyful and useful. It will help to make others more thankful and encouraged and godly and pliable and confident. And it will bring glory to God.

We refer to some people, some days or events or things, as unforgettable. I wonder what in your life you have considered unforgettable? Memory can be erased by the rush of events, by the passage of time, by the loss of interest. Christian, do you remember God's blessings in your life? Can you? Will you? Will you help others around you to do so as well? It might be the best thing you can do to help them—and yourself. Forgetfulness of God's grace is one of the greatest tools in the enemy's war against our souls.

Pray that God would help you get to know others, to care for them, to be observant of their lives, and to be kind to them. Help them to carry their burdens and sorrows by reminding them of God's good work in their life. Help to give them heart for the fight that we are called to in this life. That is how Paul begins this letter, and it would not be a bad thing for you to begin doing the same in others' lives today. Call to their attention evidences of God's grace for their good and for God's glory. Answer God's repeated call in Scripture to remember.

2

DIVISION

1 CORINTHIANS 1:10—3:23

Division is always a hot topic of conversation. In 2005 Hurricane Katrina made race and poverty divides painfully obvious. In the wake of the devastation, commentators referenced the delicate social fabric of our nation and how the evacuation plans in New Orleans effectively ignored the need to evacuate the poorest 10 percent of the population, those who do not own cars and had no money to pay for transportation out. Is such neglect of the poor endemic to our society? If so, how does it threaten the "social fabric"? Division means conflict, and conflict means suffering and sadness. We do not like division, but it is something we ought to discuss in our sphere of influence, in our callings as citizens and employees.

Ultimately we face an even more important division, one that is closer to home for Christians—division in the church. Christ himself prayed in John 17 that his followers would be "one," and from that point on, unity has been of paramount concern for Christians. One of the chief objections that the Roman Catholic Church had against the Protestant Reformation was the proposed loss of ecclesiastical authority, which was thought to hold the church together. Yet I think that we can say, almost half a millennium later, that their concern was unfounded. Today there is worldwide unity in the gospel.

Nevertheless, we still face and must address the issues that cause disunity in our local congregations. Issues arise, personalities conflict, sins are committed. Resolution can be difficult work, and fighting our corner and backing our guy can be so much more immediately appealing. Whether or not you see in your own congregation the extent of the unity problem that Paul addresses in this letter to the Corinthians, I think you will find significant the passage before us now, 1 Corinthians 1:10–3:23, as we think about how we are to relate to one another in a local church.

The situation in Corinth was an understandable one. The church—just a few years old—was full of people used to hearing professional speakers on the city streets. As one public speaker after another rose up in Corinth, passersby would latch on to the ones they most enjoyed and become committed to championing their cause publicly, whether it was financial gain, religious prestige, or political control, and this cultural practice threatened to engulf the church.

This threat is the first problem in a long list of problems within the church that Paul addressed in his letter. After encouraging them (1 Cor. 1:1–9), Paul addressed the situation of partisanship around personalities, exposing that the root of the problem stretched down to the very core of the gospel.

Paul begins tackling the problem with this command: "I appeal to you, brothers, in the name of our Lord Jesus Christ, that all of you agree with one another so that there may be no divisions among you and that you may be perfectly united in mind and thought" (1 Cor. 1:10). Indeed, it is this command for perfect unity and an exploration of the divisions preventing it that take up the first three chapters of 1 Corinthians—almost one-fifth of the entire epistle.

Unity is important because its shape and center—what we are united around—show what we are about. However, a concern for unity all too often becomes an end in itself. When it does, ironically, it causes endless discussions about unity and becomes an ever-elusive goal. A. W. Tozer made this point:

> One hundred pianos all tuned to the same fork are automatically tuned to each other. They are of one accord by being tuned, not to each other, but to another standard to which each one must individually bow. So one hundred worshippers met together, each one looking away to Christ, are in heart nearer

to each other than they could possibly be were they to become 'unity' conscious and turn their eyes away from God to strive for closer fellowship.[1]

But in Corinth the problem was not false unity; it was, rather, a destructive divisiveness. Paul had learned of the situation through friends in Corinth: "My brothers, some from Chloe's household have informed me that there are quarrels among you" (v. 11). As Paul heard about the nature of the divisions, his concern grew. He recognized the importance of dealing with the issues at stake—blasphemy, heresy, pride, folly, immaturity, rebellion, self-deception, and judgment. They were all serious issues. All of this challenged the church at the very root of its being, so Paul gives them—and us—seven reasons for unity.

Godly Unity Displays Christ

The first reason Paul gives for the importance of agreement among the Corinthian believers is that godly unity displays Christ. He writes:

> What I mean is this: One of you says, "I follow Paul"; another, "I follow Apollos"; another, "I follow Cephas"; still another, "I follow Christ." Is Christ divided? Was Paul crucified for you? Were you baptized into the name of Paul? I am thankful [thank God] that I did not baptize any of you except Crispus and Gaius, so no one can say that you were baptized into my name. (Yes, I also baptized the household of Stephanas; beyond that, I don't remember if I baptized anyone else.) (1 Cor. 1:12–16)

Paul poses a question: "Is Christ divided?" (v. 13). Their division created a lie about what Christ is like. Christ is not divided. The Corinthians were to be united in order to display the truth about Christ in the midst of a very secular city. Corinth was full of secular orators, eloquent men who made their livings by giving speeches and teaching classes. A number of the Christian teachers were apparently quite eloquent, like Apollos from Alexandria. Some of the Christians in Corinth were partisan, even divisive, apparently touting their loyalties to the various teachers as if they were peddlers selling their competing wares. Among the many problems that this caused was the miscommunication about Christ, who is not divided.

Archaeologists have found remains of religious objects in Corinth with inscriptions such as "I belong to Aphrodite" and "I belong to Demeter," among others. Such inscription practices crept into the church with the result that

Christians were making Christianity seem like nothing more than a new line of religious products.

My friends, let me be clear about what Christianity teaches. There is one God who has made us all. We have sinned against him—we have done what we have wanted rather than what he has told us to do. We have rebelled against him, and so he is rightly committed to punishing us, as our sins deserve. But, in his great mercy, he came in Christ—fully God and fully man—and lived a perfect life with no punishment of his own to bear. Yet Christ died on the cross to pay the penalty for the sins of all those who would ever turn from their sins and trust in him. He rose to new life, and he offers us new life as well, if we will turn from our sins and trust him. We lay hold of Christ savingly by believing in this message and having faith in him. This message is the important thing—not which book or friend or minister you may first hear it from.

My Christian brothers and sisters, I hope and pray that you value unity in the church, and that you see that godly unity does display Christ. There can be a wrong attachment to ministers: "this one is more passionate"; "that one has more educational experience"; or "this other one has led me into a mystical experience." None of these is the correct basis for respecting a man's ministry. We love the minister as we love the Christ he serves. Paul answered a practical problem—division—by turning to theology; he did not begin doing a comparison of the ministers. He went to the heart of the issue. Godly unity displays Christ.

Godly Unity Exalts the Cross

Paul gives a second reason for the Corinthians to be perfectly united: Godly unity exalts the cross (1:17–25). Division on the basis of what is pleasing to worldly appetites in terms of how the preaching or teaching is done promotes the messenger and obscures the cross. That is why the kind of unity toward which Paul exhorts the Corinthians is a unity around the gospel of Christ and his cross, a message that was repulsive to the ancient world. Paul writes:

> Since in the wisdom of God the world through its wisdom did not know him, God was pleased through the foolishness of what was preached to save those who believe. Jews demand miraculous signs and Greeks look for wisdom, but we preach Christ crucified: a stumbling block to Jews and foolishness to Gentiles, but to those whom God has called, both Jews and Greeks, Christ the power of God and the wisdom of God. For the foolishness of God is

wiser than man's wisdom, and the weakness of God is stronger than man's strength. (vv. 21–25)

No one was looking for the one true God to be incarnate and to bear our sins as a substitute by dying the death of an outcast traitor. So when the church begins to peddle a message by what pleases the world, of course the true gospel will be deemphasized or compromised, if not actually replaced. Polls are not always reliable guides to the truth, are they?

When a church divides in the way this church was dividing, it lies about what Christ has done. It seems to make our sin and his death smaller matters than they really are. Polished, positive preachers are no substitutes for Christ crucified. We must recognize that the world thinks the Christian message is foolish because Christ was rejected and crucified.

My brothers and sisters, treasure the cross. Meditate on how God has loved us. Explore its wonders, work to understand it, and share about it clearly with others. Realize that God himself must move on the heart of someone to believe this message. Paul makes clear that by our own human wisdom, we never come to know God.

Friends, if you find yourself moving to another community and looking for a new church, look for this most of all—the clear preaching of Christ and him crucified. Look for it in the hymns and prayers and in the preaching. Look for a commitment to faithfully offensive evangelism—evangelism that makes clear that we do not save ourselves, but that our only hope is trusting in God alone through Christ alone.

As the Heidelberg Catechism asks, "How many things are necessary for you to know that you in this comfort may live and die happily?" (Q.2), and it provides this answer: "Three; the first, how great my sins and misery are; the second, how I am delivered from all my sins and misery; the third, how I am to be thankful to God for such deliverance." This deliverance came in a way the world would have never guessed. Paul, drawing from Isaiah the prophet, makes clear that God destroyed the wisdom of the wise at the cross (1 Cor. 1:19). Any true church unity is unity around that fact. Godly unity exalts the cross; worldly divisions obscure it.

Godly Unity Expresses Humility

Paul gives a third reason to the Corinthians to be perfectly united and to agree together: godly unity expresses humility (1 Cor. 1:26–31). The divisions in the Corinthian church were ridiculous in light of their history:

Consider your calling, brothers: not many of you were wise according to worldly standards, not many were powerful, not many were of noble birth. But God chose what is foolish in the world to shame the wise; God chose what is weak in the world to shame the strong; God chose what is low and despised in the world, even things that are not, to bring to nothing things that are, so that no human being might boast in the presence of God. (1 Cor. 1:26–29)

Dividing the church over which teachers were more prestigious was utterly foolish. The whole gospel we profess as Christians trashes this world's estimates and judgments. Paul reminds the Corinthians that they were nothing to write home about (v. 26). They should know just by looking in the mirror, Paul warns them, that a status-oriented message is false. It is a historical fact, he argues, that God chooses the foolish and weak. Anyone who wants to follow Christ must begin that way. You must begin by realizing that you will never find out how much God *is* till you realize how much you *are not*.

I remember reading of a Salvation Army leader who gave this testimony on his deathbed: "I deserve to be damned; I deserve to be in hell; *but God interfered*." If you are a Christian, that is your story. It is a story that exalts the cross and humbles us. We must confess that we need to be saved, that we are the lowly that Paul writes about in verse 28. Not until we get down low like that—down low like Jonah in the belly of the great fish—do we realize, as Jonah put it, "Salvation comes from the LORD" (Jonah 2:9).

Why does God choose the lowly? He does so to prevent our boasting of the sort that brought about just the kind of division that was going on between the Corinthians and that had gone on among Jesus' own disciples when they argued among themselves about who was the greatest. Paul states that we Christians are in Christ only because of God, not because of anything in us (v. 30). All the benefits Paul speaks of here in this verse—righteousness, holiness, redemption—come through God's wisdom in Christ. Such things are not native to us and our own virtue, which is why Paul goes on to quote Jeremiah, who said, "Let the one who boasts, boast in the Lord" (v. 31 ESV; see Jer. 9:24). When your boasting is only in God, it is hard to get proud and defensive and divisive. Regularly work to humble yourself by comparing what you deserve with what you have been given.

When our churches are doing well, it is a cause for humility, not pride, because God is behind it. Therefore, the goal of our gatherings is to humble ourselves and to exalt Christ. Godly unity expresses humility.

Godly Unity Shows Wisdom

A fourth reason Paul gives for godly unity in a church is that it shows wisdom (1 Cor. 2:1–16).

Godly unity shows wisdom. God's wisdom, which is far different from this world's wisdom, is the example to follow. Godly wisdom will not be found by making earthly distinctions, which is why the divisions in the Corinthian church were futile. It should have been obvious how God had worked through them—he worked through their weakness. Paul urges the Corinthian believers to look at him as an example. He, too, was unimpressive to the world. His ministry was a demonstration of God's wisdom, not worldly wisdom. God's wisdom is different from this world's, and understanding it comes not by our virtue or cleverness but by God's gift.

In Paul's day, secular orators entered the city of Corinth, praised it eloquently, and told of all that they had done so that the rich would be impressed and become their patrons. Their aim was to gain a reputation, and they did so primarily by their method of speech and by the particular words they used. Contrarily, Paul preached a message that was folly to the world—the cross of Christ. Furthermore, Paul was weak in his person. In fact, we learn from Acts 18 that Paul, on his first visit to Corinth, was scared. God himself spoke to Paul in a vision one night in order to encourage him. Paul's preaching was weak, too, at least in terms of human wisdom. Its strength lay in the fact that God had empowered Paul's preaching to convert the Corinthians and to change their lives and establish the church.

Paul tells us that he deliberately let his weakness show so that the Corinthians' faith would be based on God rather than on him (2:5). Isn't it wonderful to know that the reality of God's power will never be overturned by a clever argument? The Christian message is not the wisdom of the streets. It came into the world in a most remarkable manner.

Paul emphasizes that the wisdom he taught was of God, that it was eternal, that it was secret, and that it told of great good from God to us (1 Cor. 2:7). Doesn't that sound like wisdom you want to know more about? You won't find it in this world anywhere else. Paul writes, "None of the rulers of this age understood it, for if they had, they would not have crucified the Lord of glory" (v. 8). Paul gives this as evidence that the world does not understand God's wisdom. Understanding God's wisdom is a gift, which is why we pray for the Holy Spirit of God to help us understand. "The natural person does not accept the things of the Spirit of God, for they are folly to him, and he is not able to understand them because they are spiritually discerned" (v. 14 ESV). We are by nature blind to the beauty of God's truth.

My brothers and sisters, do not take this wisdom for granted. Attend church regularly. Give yourself to studying God's Word in order to grow in true wisdom. May God forgive us for and turn us from our self-satisfaction and complacency. We want to cultivate a self-consciousness about our oddness as Christians in this world, and we want to do it as a united body. Godly unity within a church shows true godly wisdom.

Godly Unity Evidences Spiritual Maturity

Paul gives a fifth reason for unity in the congregation: godly unity evidences spiritual maturity. Paul writes, "Brothers, I could not address you as spiritual but as worldly—mere infants in Christ. I gave you milk, not solid food, for you were not yet ready for it. Indeed, you are still not ready. You are still worldly. For since there is jealousy and quarreling among you, are you not worldly? Are you not acting like mere men?" (1 Cor. 3:1–3). These verses show us that godly unity evidences spiritual maturity. Conversely, the divisions in the church at Corinth reveal a spiritual immaturity.

Paul writes to them here as to spiritual infants, or worldly people, because they just didn't seem ready for anything more. This was a weakness they were culpable for. We do not blame a three-year-old for not carrying on a mature conversation, but the same argument cannot be made about the Corinthians. They had had every opportunity to grow much in Christ. Paul had lived among them for a year and a half. It seems that Peter (Cephas) had been there as well. Apollos—apparently a remarkable Christian teacher—had been among them and may have still been when Paul wrote this letter. The Corinthians had received enough teaching to know better than to have the kinds of divisions they were having. They were living by the secular norms of Corinth, and their jealousy and quarrelling proved it.

From these verses, some have developed the idea of the "carnal Christian." A carnal Christian is supposedly someone who chooses to live a quasi-committed Christian lifestyle, a sort of low-option, no-cross version of Christian discipleship. But I think that this is a perversion of Paul's teaching. He is deliberately creating a contradiction in terms with this idea of "worldly brothers," "mere men," and "carnal Christians." Paul is calling attention to their troubling state to shame them out of it. He is calling them to grow up, to fish or cut bait, to act decisively. That is what his words about spiritual immaturity are meant to do.

What this means is of the utmost importance for people who have ingested the teaching about carnal Christians. It may mean that some people who thought they were converted years ago, simply because they prayed a prayer, may need to examine themselves. They might find that they have never been truly interested in spiritual things and in growing as a Christian. A true Christian wants to mature spiritually to be more like Christ. Oh, my friends, beware this carnal Christian trap! Brothers and sisters, take note of what helps and what hinders your growth as a Christian and live accordingly. Take responsibility for pursuing Christ hard. Resolve to follow him. And do not be surprised that doing so will take some effort on your part.

In the church I pastor, we are committed to working with one another for the long term, over years. We do not teach that carnal Christianity is an optional way to live. Our evangelism course is called "Two Ways to Live," a title representative of the fact that we as a church are committed to the biblical teaching that there is no saving faith apart from genuine repentance for our sins. The unity to which Paul was calling the Corinthians comes as the result of spiritual maturity and gives evidence of it.

Godly Unity Reflects a Submission to God

The sixth reason Paul gives for the need for unity is that it reflects submission to God. Paul writes, "For when one says, 'I follow Paul,' and another, 'I follow Apollos,' are you not mere men?" (1 Cor. 3:4). The divisions in the Corinthian church were essentially an attack on God himself. What Paul recounts here reveals that they were thinking about the ministry and the church in a godless way. So he sets out an argument:

> What, after all, is Apollos? And what is Paul? Only servants, through whom you came to believe—as the Lord has assigned to each his task. I planted the seed, Apollos watered it, but God made it grow. So neither he who plants nor he who waters is anything, but only God, who makes things grow. The man who plants and the man who waters have one purpose, and each will be rewarded according to his own labor. For we are God's fellow workers; you are God's field, God's building. (vv. 5–9)

Paul argues that God is the one who directs the various workmen he employs, and he has a right to do this because God is the one who founded the church (vv. 10–15). He set the foundation on Christ alone. All work will be judged not on its superficial appearance but on how consistent it is with this foundation. Paul concludes his argument by showing (vv. 16–20) that all he has said thus far points simply to the fact that God owns the church. We, that is, the local church, are God's temple. Therefore, he says, "If anyone destroys God's temple, God will destroy him; for God's temple is sacred, and you are that temple" (v. 17).

The church in Corinth was in danger of being destroyed by, among other things, ungodly division. No one will ever succeed in destroying the church universal; Christ has promised that, and history has borne out the truth of that promise in striking ways. But local congregations can be wounded and even killed. God said that he himself will destroy such a person.

Perhaps you have not considered before now the importance of Christ to the church—he is our foundation. Perhaps you have not considered the importance of the church to God—it is his, and he will have it and protect it, even against you if need be. Godly unity reflects a submission to God, recognition of his ownership of the church, and respect for his wishes.

Godly Unity Comes from Treasuring God's Promises

The seventh and final reason Paul gives here for why unity is important is that it is linked to God's promises: "So then, no more boasting about men! All things are yours, whether Paul or Apollos or Cephas or the world or life or death or the present or the future—all are yours, and you are of Christ, and Christ is of God" (3:21–23).

Paul teaches that the kind of godly unity he is calling for comes from treasuring God's promises. Because of those promises, the divisions in the Corinthian church are totally unnecessary. Paul and Apollos are theirs, along with everything else. In other words, there is no need for divisiveness because everything God has promised is already theirs. Earlier in the letter Paul wrote:

> I always thank God for you because of his grace given you in Christ Jesus. For in him you have been enriched in every way—in all your speaking and in all your knowledge—because our testimony about Christ was confirmed in you. Therefore you do not lack any spiritual gift as you eagerly wait for our Lord Jesus Christ to be revealed. (1:4–7)

Christ has enriched Christians in every way so that all the faithful Christian teachers and what they promise are ours already. They are ours, he says, because they are God's, and God is ours through Christ.

Oh, my friends, this world's pleasures are not what they are cracked up to be. Realize their emptiness while you still can, before it is too late. Loss and death were hard for Christ, yet he had confidence in the joy set before him more so than anyone else in history. How hard must suffering be for those who know nothing of any joys to come, and indeed, who think this world is all there is! How much harder still the reality of eternity without God, a reality that will make them long for the worst of this world's sufferings.

Christian, we are owned by Christ. We are his property. Meditate on your riches in him. Explore them. Set your heart upon them. We do that by the hymns we sing, by our prayers and conversations, our teaching and preaching. We can only give ourselves away in this life as we should when we remember and believe and treasure the promises coming to us in the next life as God's much-loved, long-lost, and now dearly adopted children. Think on these things, and the little slights will disappear, the sting of disappointment will be softened, and even the pain of gaping griefs will dull as the joys of God's eternal presence stretching out before you begin to dawn on your soul. Godly unity comes from treasuring God's promises.

Conclusion

In 1723, a young pastor of a church in Manhattan, Jonathan Edwards, preached a sermon called "The Nakedness of Job." He described wealthy Job's sudden losses, which included even the lives of his children. And then he turned to how we ought to respond to such losses in contrast to how the world responds:

> Perhaps, when you read the history of Job, you read it as a strange thing that happened but once in the world; but, for the time to come, read it as a thing that happens daily, and frequently, for every man at death is as much deprived of all his worldly goods as Job was. . . . The history of Job is only a shadow of death; it is no more than happens to every man in the world. . . . Such is the folly of the world. They pursue violently after the world, slave and tire themselves for a little of it, are exceeding anxious and careful about it. Their minds are gnawn with care and anxiety; they undergo abundance of difficulties for it, and will often violate their consciences, disobey their God, and go very near hellfire—so near as to scorch them—come so near to the pit that their feet

are every moment ready to slip. When they lose the world, they mourn as if they had met with a loss that it is impossible should be repaired either in this world or the next, and when they have got a little of the world, they please themselves with the thoughts of it as much as if they were sure they could never lose it, neither by death nor otherwise. . . . Before, they were careless and at ease, as if death were not wont to come into their parts of the world."[2]

Hurricane Katrina hit the Louisiana coastline in 2005 and pierced the satanic illusion of this world's permanence. The price was high. For untold numbers it cost them everything. For still more it cost them family, friends, home, possessions, and various other treasures. The event brings to mind a parable Jesus told, a parable that is eerily contemporary:

"Everyone who hears these words of mine and puts them into practice is like a wise man who built his house on the rock. The rain came down, the streams rose, and the winds blew and beat against that house; yet it did not fall, because it had its foundation on the rock. But everyone who hears these words of mine and does not put them into practice is like a foolish man who built his house on the sand. The rain came down, the streams rose, and the winds blew and beat against that house, and it fell with a great crash." (Matt. 7:24–27)

Biloxi and Gulfport and even New Orleans are rising again. But there is no recovery from the crash Jesus describes in his parable. I pray that all of us will be aware of the truth of our own state, that we will look to unity in our congregations and from it to the great gospel of the crucified Christ it reflects. I pray also that we will look to our own treasures to see if our hearts are founded on the Rock, Christ, or if we have built our lives and loves in more dangerous places. The storm that hit New Orleans was costly enough; don't wait for the final storm to blow through your soul. Prepare before that time. For us as a church—and for you as an individual—build on the Rock, the Rock that is Christ and him crucified.

3

IMPOSTORS

1 CORINTHIANS 4

Were the ministers real or were they fake? It was hard to tell. They came like all the others had come. They looked like the others, maybe a little more impressive or a little more driven. They knew that they had come for a reason; they did not think the way everyone else did. They knew they would have to speak in such a way as to command respect, even obedience. But the results of their presence, their words, even their actions, would be terrible for them, and for all those around them. For a short amount of worldly glory, they and those who followed their words would be repaid by eternal grief.

Who knows what their hopes were? We can speculate. We can guess that they wanted to accomplish this or that. Whatever noble end they sought to achieve, they still desired to make a name for themselves. They were probably well paid, if one can ever be sufficiently paid for that kind of work.

Today is a day to think of such people. We have checks in place to catch them now, things we look for. Some things we require; other things we do not allow. No matter the checks, we still learn painfully by trial and error.

The place of the tragedy was a world-class city. The stakes were high, very high. The duped were a bunch of easily led people. And the solution, the hope, was some written instructions, a not so impressive speaker, and God.

The problem was that people were being fooled, misled, and deceived. A few were prospering, but the gospel was being obscured from view, silenced by a seemingly effective, substitute message. The true congregation was facing—in a word—*impostors*. The solution Paul puts forward is his first letter to the Corinthians, complete with a promise of a visit to come. We now turn to examine the fourth chapter of Paul's epistle.

In 1 Corinthians 4 there is a striking contrast between the real ministers of Christ and the fake ones, the impostors. In this passage we find three marks of a real minister.

A Cross-centered Message

The first mark of a real minister is his cross-centered message. "So then, men ought to regard us as servants of Christ and as those entrusted with the secret things of God," Paul writes (v. 1). The secret things of God—that is what a real minister is all about. Paul takes up this subject here after warning the Corinthians against dividing over competing loyalties to different ministers or preachers. They are not the ones appointed to judge who's who:

> Now it is required that those who have been given a trust must prove faithful. I care very little if I am judged by you or by any human court; indeed, I do not even judge myself. My conscience is clear, but that does not make me innocent. It is the Lord who judges me. Therefore judge nothing before the appointed time; wait till the Lord comes. He will bring to light what is hidden in darkness and will expose the motives of men's hearts. At that time each will receive his praise from God. (vv. 2–5)

Paul saw an important principle at stake here: it is God's prerogative, and his alone, to judge, because everything is his gift. Everything is done to his ends, his purposes. Ministers of the gospel, especially, are stewards of God's mysteries, his secret things—the gospel. A steward is not an owner but one who is entrusted with someone else's property. God has entrusted his servants with the message of the crucified Messiah.

Paul wanted the Corinthians to understand that these servants, ministers, are judged by whether they are faithful to their master. Their master was not the Corinthian congregation, and it certainly was not the worldly standards that seemed to control them. Even the apostles were ministers, not masters. They were fundamentally servants not of the Corinthians but of Christ. As Matthew Henry put it, "They had no authority to propagate their own fancies, but to spread Christian faith."

We Christians today are to view ministers as servants and stewards, too. "Steward" is a great name for a minister. Ministers do not own the church; it is not theirs. Ministers are God's employees. He is their boss. They work ultimately for him, and the main task he has given them is making known the secret things of God, the gospel of the crucified Messiah.

What is the one thing such a steward is called to do above all else? A steward must be faithful. "It is required that those who have been given a trust must prove faithful" (v. 2). Of course, Paul's statement was an implicit condemnation of any unfaithful teacher among them. According to 1 Peter 4:10, all Christians are stewards, but ministers especially must be trustworthy. We teachers of God's Word will be held to a stricter judgment (see James 3:1). Ministers are like bankers, entrusted with a great deposit. We ministers of the Word must be faithful in our work because of the great value of what has been committed to us. We are not concerned to be original but rather reliable, as we recount the gospel of Christ crucified. No one—not the Corinthians, or believers today, or ministers, or even Paul himself—has the authority to change the message.

Christians know that the gospel message is not always popular. It was not created using focus groups and strategic polling research to convey maximum appeal. The message of forgiveness through faith in Christ crucified and risen and returning to judge is offensive to our pride. "I don't need Jesus Christ living for me, and certainly not dying for me!" we think. But we do need him.

When Paul writes, "I care very little if I am judged by you or by any human court; indeed, I do not even judge myself. My conscience is clear, but that does not make me innocent. It is the Lord who judges me," he isn't saying that self-examination is wrong. In fact, he calls for it later in this letter (1 Cor. 9:24–27; cf. 2 Cor. 13:5), but our self-assessment of a clear conscience simply is not ultimate. Self-esteem cannot be the final arbiter of judgment because we esteem ourselves too highly. We are called to make provisional judgments (Matt. 7:6; 1 Corinthians 5), but no mere human can be our ultimate judge, because, as Paul says, we all will be judged by the Lord (cf. 1 Cor. 2:10–16).

Do you see the freedom here in knowing the identity of your ultimate judge, that there is only one, and that he can be well-disposed toward you? Assure yourself of God's verdict through Christ, and you will have little regard for the judgments of others. But remember that you cannot please God if you live to please men. A true minister of Christ, Paul says here, is living to please Christ, the one and only coming Judge. The time will come for the ultimate judgment, but not now, and not by the Corinthians: "Therefore judge nothing before the appointed time; wait till the Lord comes. He will bring to light what is hidden in darkness and will expose the motives of men's hearts. At that time each will receive his praise from God" (4:5; cf. 3:13).

The Corinthians were tempted to wrongly esteem teachers who were impressive by worldly standards, their external appearance, or their striking manner. But Paul reveals that making prideful, worldly comparisons between one Christian teacher and another, whether Paul, Apollos, or someone else, is incredibly inappropriate. All true Christian teachers have been commissioned by the same Master with the same message for the same purpose—the glory of God by the proclaiming of his reign. To allow partisan splits, as the Corinthians were doing, was to lose sight of the value of the message, allowing it to become obscured by the messenger and the particular gifts one teacher had over another. Then as now, once that begins to happen, following a particular messenger beyond faithfulness to the Word of God is not far behind.

Paul continues, "Now, brothers, I have applied these things to myself and Apollos for your benefit, so that you may learn from us the meaning of the saying, 'Do not go beyond what is written.' Then you will not take pride in one man over against another" (1 Cor. 4:6). Little is known about the origin of this quotation, "Do not go beyond what is written," beyond the fact that apparently it was well known. Most likely it was simply a reference to the phrase "it is written," which was used to introduce Old Testament quotations. Paul is encouraging the Corinthians to be committed to the message and to cherish faithfulness to the cross in their preachers.

We who are ministers should be careful to remember that we are servants and stewards. We are to be esteemed in our role only as instruments pointing to Christ, and we must be faithful to deliver this message. With this understanding, Paul and Apollos were not in competition, as Paul explains carefully to the Corinthians in the opening chapters of this letter. Because, as he says, "For who makes you different from anyone else? What do you have that you did not receive? And if you did receive it, why do you boast as though you did not?" (4:7). Everything you and your various teachers have, you have received from God.

Friends, the three questions Paul poses in verse 7 have been some of the most important questions in the Bible down through the history of

Christianity. From Augustine to Martin Luther, God has used this verse to powerfully affect people and humble them and to exalt himself. Let this question echo in your own soul for a little while: "What do you have that you did not receive?"

The last Sunday night of his life, John Knox reported that he was tempted by Satan to trust in himself and to rejoice, or boast, in himself, "but" said Knox to his servant, "I repulsed him with this sentence: 'What do [I] have that [I] did not receive?'" Remember what Paul said in 1:31 about boasting: "Let him who boasts, boast in the Lord." What do we have more to boast about than the cross of Christ, by which God has satisfied his love and his justice, his mercy and his holiness, and displayed it to all the world as he saves all who trust in him? A real minister has this at the center of his message.

A Cross-centered Life

The second mark of a real minister is his cross-centered life. Paul writes, "For it seems to me that God has put us apostles on display at the end of the procession, like men condemned to die in the arena. We have been made a spectacle to the whole universe, to angels as well as to men" (v. 9). Here Paul is describing his experience and that of the other apostles, which stands in stark contrast to the Corinthians' claims of prosperity (v. 8). As we will see, Paul uses some very sharp, ironic questions in this section of the letter to deflate the Corinthians' pride and to reorient them to the cross and to Christ's teaching about true discipleship.

Heavy irony and a number of sarcastic statements are not Paul's normal way of teaching, but it is not outside the bounds of appropriate communication sometimes. In fact, irony could be particularly useful in helping the Corinthians to see how these false apostles had confused them, how topsy-turvy their view of the Christian life had become. "Already you have all you want! Already you have become rich! You have become kings—and that without us! How I wish that you really had become kings so that we might be kings with you!" (v. 8). Can you see what Paul is doing here? He is mocking the Corinthians' prosperity, whether real or imagined. Either way, it is clear that many in the Corinthian church were feeling confident and fulfilled. But regardless of how they might have felt, Paul calls them back to reality by pointing to the obvious fact that they are not kings. It is likely that Paul was addressing the notion, some false teaching, that the promised, future glorified state was already upon them.

Paul's life was a little more humble than theirs, it seems. He uses the images of the processions and the spectacles to communicate how he feels (v. 9). In military processions, the prisoners came last in line, and very last of all came the lowest in rank and the most despised. That, Paul said, had been his experience in life, which was very different from the "reigning" posture that the Corinthians were claiming for themselves. The military processions marched to the theater in Corinth, which seated eighteen thousand people, with the most wretched prisoner left for the last show, the last "spectacle" of the day. Paul likens himself to that spectacle.

How different this life is from the notion of spiritual kingship, which the Corinthians were being taught by the impostors. Paul employs sarcasm again: "We are fools for Christ, but you are so wise in Christ! We are weak, but you are strong! You are honored, we are dishonored!" (v. 10). The Corinthians saw themselves as wise, strong, and worthy of honor, whereas Paul understood that he was foolish (in the world's eyes), weak, and dishonored. The deceived ones in the Corinthian church had cobbled together some illusions, replacing the cross as the center of the Christian life with something much more palatable. Matthew Henry thinks they were self-deceived: "Those do not commonly know themselves best who think best of themselves."

If you think you are basically a great person, and that anytime your conscience stirs it is simply some imbalance in your self-esteem, some feeling to be ignored or suppressed, then you are not following Christ. The Christian message of a crucified Christ calls us to a different goal. We are no longer concerned with the world's wisdom, a world that made the decision to crucify Christ. We no longer live for what a world that opposes God calls "strength." We're not captivated by applause and honor from those who have rejected Jesus, who is the wisdom of God. My friend, if you have been living for worldly wisdom and honor, are you beginning to notice how unsatisfying it is? There is a better way: Christ rejected and put to death on the cross actually saves us by his death on the cross:

> "Surely he took up our infirmities and carried our sorrows, yet we considered him stricken by God, smitten by him, and afflicted. But he was pierced for our transgressions, he was crushed for our iniquities; the punishment that brought us peace was upon him, and by his wounds we are healed. We all, like sheep, have gone astray, each of us has turned to his own way; and the LORD has laid on him the iniquity of us all. (Isa. 53:4–6)

If the One whom we follow was stricken, smitten, and afflicted, if he was pierced and crushed and punished and wounded, then we can't be too surprised that some of that may happen to us in this world—especially to his ministers, not because by our death we bear sin, but because in our lives, we live in a way this world rejects.

In Corinth eloquent orators were prized. They were celebrated and honored and well paid. It seems that some of this had crept into the church; men were being honored not for giving the message of the cross, but for how well they presented themselves, regardless of their actual message. True ministers of Christ are happy to be despised, if, by their being despised, somehow the gospel is displayed. Most of us are familiar with the bargain on which Jim Elliot based his life: "He is no fool who gives what he cannot keep to gain what he cannot lose." Remember what Paul said back earlier in the letter: "The foolishness of God is wiser than man's wisdom, and the weakness of God is stronger than man's strength" (1 Cor. 1:25). True ministers of Christ and his cross have experienced this and are confident of it.

Paul shared in the rejection of Christ in his own life: "To this very hour we go hungry and thirsty, we are in rags, we are brutally treated, we are homeless" (v. 11). Paul uses present-tense verbs here because he was experiencing these very things at the time of his epistle. He wasn't writing from some great cathedral or from a cushy university lectureship. No, he sounds more like an evacuee here. But his hope didn't rest on anything in this world. Real ministers have their hope stored elsewhere.

Paul continues, "We work hard with our own hands. When we are cursed, we bless; when we are persecuted, we endure it; when we are slandered, we answer kindly. Up to this moment we have become the scum of the earth, the refuse of the world" (vv. 12–13). He works with his hands, preaches the gospel, experiences rejection from this world, and keeps on going, even when his clothes are threadbare and he is bone tired. Paul worked as a tentmaker in Corinth (Acts 18:3), a profession that the Corinthians would have scorned. Well-to-do citizens of Corinth would have been embarrassed to ask their friends to come and hear someone who lived by manual labor, as Paul did. But Paul pressed on, clearly not living for the approval of this world as the false ministers were doing.

When the world cursed Paul, or persecuted him, or slandered him, they weren't taking away from him anything he expected to keep. He believed that he had no right to well-wishes from God-haters, no ultimate right to freedom or to a good name among those who rejected Christ. Paul simply responded to such opposition as Christ had taught his followers to do (see

Matt. 5:10–12; Luke 6:28) and in the way that Jesus himself had responded to his suffering: "When they hurled their insults at him, he did not retaliate; when he suffered, he made no threats. Instead, he entrusted himself to him who judges justly" (1 Pet. 2:23; cf. Luke 23:34).

Paul did not try to gloss over the opposing views of God and the world. Paul followed the One who said, "Foxes have holes and birds of the air have nests, but the Son of Man has no place to lay his head," (Luke 9:58; cf. Phil. 3:10). Paul wrote to the Romans, "If we are children, then we are heirs—heirs of God and co-heirs with Christ, if indeed we share in his sufferings in order that we may also share in his glory" (Rom. 8:17).

Brothers and sisters, the only way to follow Jesus is to die to self-interest daily. Live as Paul lived here. I don't mean that you should try to imitate his circumstances, but follow his course. Commit yourself to following Christ, regardless of whether following him cuts across desires the world says are your rights. Young people, realize that following Christ is not always the same thing as being popular with your friends. Sometimes you will have to choose between the two.

Prosperity and worldliness are not always wrong, but they are always dangerous. They can be disorienting to the Christian. We must live lives that show there are things that are worth even more than this world's prosperity and worldliness. How can you do that in your circumstances this week? And think of those who minister the Word to you. Pray that they would live lives that evidence the supremacy of Christ and his cross. Such a lifestyle is listed among the qualifications for elders. We ministers want to live a life that is different from this world, a life that tells the truth, a life that gives hope in a dying world. Real ministers live cross-centered lives.

Cross-centered Followers

Cross-centered followers are the third mark of a real minister. Paul writes, "I urge you to imitate me" (v. 16). This sums up all Paul's instructions in the first quarter of the epistle. Paul urges the Corinthians (his spiritual children) to humble themselves like the apostles (and like Christ) and to stop following the foolish ways of their worldly teachers. He warns them of the false way that at least some of them seem to be on, and he urges them to follow instead his example. It is clear here that a Christian minister is called not only to teach the gospel correctly and to live out a Christlike life, but also to lead others to do the same.

For all the severity of his language, we can see that Paul really loves these Corinthians: "I am not writing this to shame you, but to warn you, as my dear children" (v. 14). Evidently Paul realized how harsh his words might have sounded. But he loves them with fatherly love. "Even though you have ten thousand guardians in Christ, you do not have many fathers, for in Christ Jesus I became your father through the gospel" (v. 15). Paul knows and reminds them that he is uniquely their father in the gospel. Paul was the church planter of the church in Corinth, the founding father of that local congregation. There is a special regard, isn't there, for those whom God used to lead us to Christ? Paul was using that—he was using anything he could get—to dissuade these young believers from following imitation teachers and their counterfeit gospel. That is why he urges the Corinthians and others elsewhere to imitate him (v. 16; see also 11:1; Gal. 4:12; Phil. 3:17; 1 Thess. 1:6; 2 Thess. 3:7, 9; cf. Heb. 13:7). Here in this letter he holds out his arms and appeals to them, "Because I alone am your father, trust me in this, imitate me in living a cross-centered life."

Children naturally mimic their parents, but calling on people to imitate us certainly puts on the pressure—hopefully the right kind of pressure! Christian preachers are models; there's no way around it. Paul as a preacher had been a good model to the Corinthians, but other teachers were now serving as poor models.

Some time ago, I had the privilege of dining with Dr. C. Everett Koop, the former surgeon general during the Reagan administration. At one point during the meal, conversation turned to the topic of good nutrition, and a comment was made to Dr. Koop about a nutritionally dubious item he was ordering off the menu. He responded that he was paid as the surgeon general to teach, not to be an example! He was joking, of course, but there is no doubt that Christians should be examples, especially those who serve Christ as ministers of his Word. We ministers ought to be prayed for, loved, obeyed, and supported for Christ's sake, but our examples also should be followed. As a preacher, one who is at least a little aware of his own sins, I know that this is a harrowing responsibility but an unavoidable part of the job. If I am going to preach the Bible, I must seek to live, by God's grace, as an example of Christ's power in my life and as an encouragement to others along the way.

If you are not a Christian, I have great news for you. There's a better life than the one you have been living. There is a life that, while full of all the trials Paul has mentioned, has more and better friends and purpose and joy and family and reward and peace and interest and usefulness (and on and on

I could go) than you've ever imagined. The joy and peace and purpose that Christ gives is not dependent on your outward circumstances. All people want this, which is one of the reasons that books about living a purpose-driven life or having your best life now sell. Fundamentally, this good life comes through being forgiven of your sins against God and being given a reconciled relationship with your Creator.

Paul wanted the Corinthians to know this, so "for this reason I am sending to you Timothy, my son whom I love, who is faithful in the Lord. He will remind you of my way of life in Christ Jesus, which agrees with what [just as] I teach everywhere in every church" (v. 17). Paul sent Timothy to teach them faithfully how to live. I'm sure it was hard to send away such a close friend and co-laborer, especially when Paul was undergoing such personal difficulty. His sending of Timothy shows something of the depth of his love for them. He yearned that they be taught the truth about Christ and that they see Christlike teachers live out the faith before them. He wouldn't rest well until he knew that the believers in Corinth better and more fully embodied the Christianity they said they believed.

That's why he says what he does at the end of chapter 4 about his own upcoming visit, and he challenges them to be ready: "Some of you have become arrogant, as if I were not coming to you" (v. 18). He is sharp again, and he clearly means it! He is effectively ordering them to be humble. Do you realize that humility is a duty for followers of Christ? Who could be more humble than Christ? So how do you imagine that you can follow him without continuing to grow in humility? How can you think to follow him in his self-giving love without shrinking in your self-concern and growing in your concern for God and others?

Paul adds, "But I will come to you very soon, if the Lord is willing, and then I will find out not only how these arrogant people are talking, but what power they have. For the kingdom of God is not a matter of talk but of power. What do you prefer? Shall I come to you with a whip, or in love and with a gentle spirit?" (vv. 19–21). Paul is clear that he will come to investigate the claims of the arrogant among them. Paul is careful to say he will come "if the Lord is willing," as if he had James's letter (James 4:15). These words are a mark of humility.

Paul says that when he comes, he will investigate not merely the words of the opposing teachers, but also their power. God's rulership, his reign, is not merely an idea—it is what happens in peoples' lives. It is happening in the lives of many of us. Paul is challenging the Corinthians to consider the false ministers with a critical eye. Are people actually being saved through their message or are they nothing more than religious windbags? Finally, Paul warns them that if they do not respond to his gentle love, he will come with a whip, by which, of course, he means not a literal whip, but a severe reproof. This is a good reminder that both gentleness and severity are part of Christian love.

I am struck by the great combination of humility and confidence Paul displays here in his words and life, and in so doing, he becomes a model for all of us. We should all desire to be bold in helping others grow in Christ. We should risk ourselves, be willing to be misunderstood, in order to be of service to others. That's why we as a church encourage discipleship.

If you are someone who is considering full-time pastoral ministry, and you are wondering whether God may be calling you into it, realize that the desire to see people changed by the gospel of the cross of Christ—whether through evangelism or discipleship—is a normal part of the experience of those God calls into such ministry. The desire is often referred to as the external confirmation that accompanies the internal sense of God's call. Pray that others around you can confirm that God does indeed use you as something of an agent for change in people's lives. That's what Paul was challenging the Corinthians to try to find in the impostors in their midst. What counts is a cross-centered message, a cross-centered life, and cross-centered followers.

Conclusion

"Shall I come to you with a whip, or in love and with a gentle spirit?" Paul asks. The way in which the believers at Corinth would prepare for his coming would determine the nature of Paul's visit. The choice that stands before you today is very much like the choice facing the Corinthians. Your life will be intersected by God, whether through the Lord's return or your death. How will that coming be for you? Will you find yourself prepared by the truth about the cross, or will you find yourself unprepared, living as if this passing world were going to last forever?

All the splendor of the Corinthian orators traded on the pervasive lie that what matters most is what we can see and feel right now. I wonder if somehow your job title, bank account, hopes, ambitions, or possessions have deceived you into thinking that this Vanity Fair we live in is actually our enduring city. It isn't. On September 11, 2001 we got a powerful reminder of that. Even the most powerful-looking and apparently indestructible buildings can be damaged or destroyed in a short time. Just a while later the residents of the Gulf Coast were going about their business, little guessing the violent disassembling that was about to go on all around them. Closer to home, some of us have lost loved ones, even in this past week, whether in great dramas or quiet, lonely endings.

Friends, how many warnings and reminders do you need? Teachers who call you to put your heart—your all—into this life are impostors. They are lying to you. There is another home, an immortal one, that you may have. And its power streams back into this life as well, which is what Paul's life and teaching witness to. The cross is the center, but it is not the end. On through the cross of this world's rejection is the eternal acceptance of God. There is no better goal for your life than being in a loving relationship with this great and glorious God forever, regardless of what passing pleasures you may have to let go of in order to take hold of it.

4

SIN

1 CORINTHIANS 5—6

I remember seeing the television report. Gary (whose last name I never got) was being interviewed. He said, "I don't want to judge anyone. I don't want to put my hate out there." That was on March 6, 2001. He was speaking about Andy Williams, the fifteen-year-old young man who had killed two people and shot others (including Gary himself) the day before at Santana High School, in suburban San Diego, California. Would Gary have been hateful if he had said something that wounded the murderer? Was it possible for Gary to evaluate, to judge, the other young man's actions in a way that is good and right?

In today's culture, we have backed ourselves into a corner on this one. We discourage judgmental statements, but our lives require evaluations all the time. David Brooks recounted, "One young man [at Yale] said his professors had taught him how to deconstruct, disentangle, and debunk. But they hadn't actually taught him how to construct a moral argument. . . . These students were trying to form judgments, yet were blocked by the accumulated habits of non-judgmentalism."[1] We have been taught a rugged individualism, a New England transcendental self-satisfaction run amock. It is, ironically, the fashion of the day to care only about what you think while ignoring the judgments of others. You have probably heard this little jingle:

When you get what you want in your struggle for wealth
    and the world makes you king for a day,
Then go to the mirror and look at yourself
    and see what that guy (or gal) has to say.
For it isn't your father or mother or wife
    whose judgment upon you must pass,
The fellow whose verdict counts most in your life
    is the guy staring back from the glass.[2]

Of course, Christians have not always been satisfied with such a lack of clear conclusions, which is one reason that some of them have such a bad reputation in the public media. As then Congressman Coburn of Oklahoma—himself a confessing Christian—said in an interview a few years ago, "When some people hear the word 'Christian' they go 'Yuck.' People associate the word with hypocrisy. People feel judged and condemned."[3]

A number of people have observed that for some time now the best-known Bible verse is likely no longer John 3:16: "For God so loved the world that he gave his only begotten Son, that whosoever believeth in him should not perish, but have everlasting life." No, these days, it is probably Matthew 7:1: "Judge not, that ye be not judged" (KJV).

If that is truly the case—if we are living in a day when even Christianity is being repackaged to present a God without wrath bringing people without sin into a kingdom without judgment through the ministrations of a Christ without a cross—then what do we as Bible-believing Christians do? What should we do in our own lives and in our churches, and how can we face the challenge of sin unless we can first recognize it and call it sin?

We find a wealth of answers to these questions and others in 1 Corinthians 5 and 6. In chapter 5 we find Paul insisting that the Corinthians excommunicate a man from the church. In chapter 6 Paul explains a bit more of the principle involved in judging those inside the church. Our goal in examining these chapters is to understand some specifics of church life and some principles of how to handle sin in the church.

The Call for Church Discipline

Paul begins with specific instructions for excommunication, and he gives at least three reasons for doing so. The first reason is for the good of the believer.

For His Own Good

Paul outlines the situation in Corinth:

> It is actually reported that there is sexual immorality among you, and of a kind that does not occur even among pagans: A man has his father's wife. And you are proud! Shouldn't you rather have been filled with grief and have put out of your fellowship the man who did this? Even though I am not physically present, I am with you in spirit. And I have already passed judgment on the one who did this, just as if I were present. When you are assembled in the name of our Lord Jesus and I am with you in spirit, and the power of our Lord Jesus is present, hand this man over to Satan, so that the sinful nature may be destroyed and his spirit saved on the day of the Lord. (1 Cor. 5:1–5)

Incest was forbidden in Roman law. In fact, one could be expelled from the city of Corinth for engaging in it. Certainly in the Jewish community there were serious sanctions (including capital punishment) against anyone caught in an incestuous act (see Lev. 18:7–8, 29; Deut. 22:30). In 1 Corinthians 4, Paul had warned about judging by standards that God has not revealed. Now, here in chapter 5, we see Paul rebuking the church for *not* judging by the standards that God *has* revealed. He rebukes the Corinthians for being proud when instead they should have removed, or excommunicated, this man from their fellowship (cf. Matt. 18:15–17; Eph. 5:3, 11; 2 Thess. 3:6).

From Paul's words it is apparent that the Corinthian church welcomed the sinning believer while being fully aware of what was going on. They may even have been boasting about their acceptance of the sin itself. At very least, it is evident from Paul's rebuke that they were tolerant of the sin. They believed themselves to be so spiritual, when in reality they were committing corporate, collective sin by their inaction and by their pride in being so tolerant. The Corinthian believers' root problem was their welcoming as members into their fellowship such brazen and unrepentant sinners.

Paul had already determined the truth about this situation, and he exhorts them to officially excommunicate this man for his own good. Jesus had founded the Corinthian church, and they had taken Christ's name upon them. For that reason they had provisional authority to speak for him. Therefore, Paul said, they should "hand this man over to Satan." Paul later used this phrase in reference to two others (1 Tim. 1:20). When Paul exhorts the Corinthian Christians to deliver the sinning man to Satan, he is referring to the public removal of the church's affirmation of his salvation. He is to be handed over publicly to the worldly life that he has chosen and excluded from the believing earthly community. Such an action was not meant to express their belief that the man was unregenerate; rather, it affirmed their knowledge that he was living as if he were unregenerate, which he may therefore have been. Excommunication would not necessarily have forbidden the man to attend public services; he was simply not to be regarded as a member, and he was therefore not to participate in the privileges of membership, especially in the Lord's Supper.

It was all for his own good so that "the flesh may be destroyed and his spirit saved." Perhaps his experience would be like that of the Prodigal Son, being abandoned to exhaust his own desires and prove their insatiability. Either way, the purpose of Paul's pronouncement was for the spiritual benefit of the sinner. Dealing with sin that hasn't been isolated and exposed is difficult, much like seeing that which is invisible or hearing that which is inaudible. Friend, if you are a non-Christian, consider that we tell you about your sins as an act of love.

Brothers and sisters, we worship a holy God. He declares incest to be wrong. But whether it is incest or something else that God has declared sinful, we must not cultivate an indifference to it, in ourselves or in others, regardless of cultural acceptance of the issue. We want to love God so much that we hate the sin that he hates in ourselves and in others, which will include a willingness to confront others in hatred of sin and in love for God and them.

At Capitol Hill Baptist Church where I am a pastor, we excommunicate people for unrepentant sin, and I use the word *we* deliberately. I use the word *we* because we as a congregation teach, and we correct. We as a congregation are active in instructing through sermons and Sunday school lessons and conversations. This is called "formative discipline." But we as a congregation also are active in correcting through lovingly disagreeing and even confronting, and, if need be, excommunicating a member for unrepentant sin. In Jesus' words in Matthew 18, the final word is left to the assembly as a whole. So Paul's instructions here. Paul's command is not directed to the elders but to the congregation as a whole. The entire congregation has a responsibility not to tolerate unrepentant sin. We pray that we can be a church where this is done for the good of the person trapped in sin, and part of that involves a commitment to join together in opposing the sin, even if that means temporarily opposing ourselves. Excommunicate this man, Paul says, for his own good.

For a Pure Church

The second reason Paul calls the church to excommunicate this man is for the sake of purity in the church:

> Your boasting is not good. Don't you know that a little yeast works through the whole batch of dough? Get rid of the old yeast that you may be a new batch without yeast—as you really are. For Christ, our Passover lamb, has been sacrificed. Therefore let us keep the Festival, not with the old yeast, the yeast of malice and wickedness, but with bread without yeast, the bread of sincerity and truth. (vv. 6–8)

Their boasting revealed that they were unaware of the corrupting nature of sin. At the Passover, all leaven was removed from the homes (see Ex. 12:15). Leaven was commonly used as an image for sin because of its spreading nature.

Paul was pointing out here that the entire community is endangered by indifference to continued, unrepentant sin. The man's sin is heinous enough, but it is the church's lack of discipline that has Paul yelling through this letter. The man's sin was a single serious infection, but the church's lack of discipline a complete failure of the immune system. We see here the spreading infection that sin is among those who tolerate it. Sin that no one deals with becomes sin that everyone will have to deal with.

Paul reminds the Corinthians that because of Christ's death they are already pure: "Get rid of the old yeast that you may be a new batch without yeast—as you really are. For Christ, our Passover lamb, has been sacrificed" (v. 7). Nevertheless, as Christians they are called to contribute the unleavened bread to the Passover feast. "Therefore let us keep the Festival, not with the old yeast, the yeast of malice and wickedness, but with bread without yeast, the bread of sincerity and truth" (v. 8). The way to do this, Paul says, is by getting the leaven of sin out of their church. The completed feast is before them—the Lamb has been slain. But the feast awaits their participation.

Friends, the purity of the church is not an unattractive prudishness but rather a wonderful, winsome, haunting, compelling beauty that Christians are called to reflect in their churches. Our lives and actions ought to portray the attractiveness of Christ to unbelievers and everyone around us. Brothers and sisters, consider carefully how much God has loved you in Christ. His only Son has become your Passover Lamb, willingly becoming the sacrifice—your sacrifice. One of my favorite devotional books is Spurgeon's *Morning and Evening:*

Every firstborn creature must be the Lord's; but since the donkey was unclean, it could not be presented in sacrifice. What then? Should it be allowed to go free from the universal law? By no means. God allows for no exceptions. The donkey is His due, but He will not accept it; He will not void the claim, but yet He cannot be pleased with the victim. As a result, no way of escape remained but redemption—the creature must be saved by the substitution of a lamb in its place; or if not redeemed, it must die. My soul, here is a lesson for you. The unclean animal is you. You are justly the property of the Lord who made you and preserves you, but you are so sinful that God will not, cannot, accept you; and it has come to this—the Lamb of God must stand in your place or you must die eternally. Let all the world know of your gratitude to that spotless Lamb who has already bled for you and so redeemed you from the fatal curse of the law. Sometimes it must have been a question for the Israelite which should die—the donkey or the lamb. Surely a good man would pause to estimate and compare. Without question there was no comparison between the value of the soul of a man and the life of the Lord Jesus, and yet the Lamb dies, and man the donkey is spared. My soul, adore the boundless love of God to you and others of the human race. Worms are purchased with the blood of the Son of the Highest! Dust and ashes are redeemed with a price far above silver and gold! What a doom was mine if plentiful redemption had not been found! The breaking of the neck of the donkey was but a momentary penalty, but who will measure the wrath to come to which no limit can be imagined? Inestimably dear is the glorious Lamb who has redeemed us from such a doom.[4]

Brothers and sisters, rejoice in God's cleansing you from your sins and giving you a fresh start as his adopted children. Rejoice in the new life he gives you. See how sin is opposed to this and fight it. Paul is here giving them another reason to excommunicate this man, not just for his own individual sake, but for the sake of the church as a whole, for its purity.

For Obedience

The third reason Paul calls the church to excommunicate this man is the Corinthians' responsibility to do so. The act is in keeping with their identity as Christians. Paul writes:

I have written you in my letter not to associate with sexually immoral people— not at all meaning the people of this world who are immoral, or the greedy and swindlers, or idolaters. In that case you would have to leave this world. But now I am writing you that you must not associate with anyone who calls himself a brother but is sexually immoral or greedy, an idolater or a slanderer, a drunkard or a swindler. With such a man do not even eat. What business is it of mine to judge those outside the church? Are you not to judge those inside? God will judge those outside. "Expel the wicked man from among you." (vv. 9–13)

Paul clearly says that the Corinthian Christians were not to associate with sexually immoral people, but he is quick to clarify that he is not referring to those outside the church, to non-Christians; Paul is writing about church members. If we were to dissociate from immoral people outside the church, we would have to establish a monastic community completely withdrawn from the world. But Paul never encourages Christians to become hermits who live in monastic retreats, such as the Amish do. Far from it! The New Testament is clear that we are not to disengage from this world. Christians are to be witnesses in the world—shining lights and gospel preachers (see Matt. 5:13–16; Acts 1:8; Phil. 2:15). Paul could not be more explicit about his meaning here: "I am writing you that you must not associate with anyone who calls himself a brother but is sexually immoral or greedy, an idolater or a slanderer, a drunkard or a swindler. With such a man do not even eat" (v. 11).

We must dissociate from such brothers and sisters because it is our business to judge those inside the church (v. 12). Doing so is our responsibility. God will judge those outside of the church (v. 13), but he has called us to act on his behalf inside the church, expelling the wicked from our midst (See Deut. 17:7; 19:19; 22:21, 24; 24:7). The church is to be distinct from society as a whole, and for us the implications involve politics, philosophy, and public moral standards. Christian involvement in the world covers every sphere of life. The church and society are not coextensive; that is, we understand that not everything that is immoral should be illegal in this world. This is partly due to the limited nature of the government's responsibility and competence. It is not the government's job to punish for lust, greed, or pride. The government is not capable of doing so. Furthermore, in a fallen world, we understand that we have no guarantee that a particular city or nation will even recognize or defend godliness and righteousness. And, it seems from the New Testament, and from Paul's words here, that the church's job is not to reform society, but to purify the church as a witness to the purity of God. In a society that distributes responsibility widely through democratic institutions, Christians have an opportunity and an obligation to work for the good of their community, but Paul says here that this is not the work of the church.

Some people rail against what they call "replacement theology" (which doesn't sound good, does it?). Here Paul takes this injunction to God's Old Testament people Israel and applies it directly to church, almost seeming to imply that the church should have realized this already! The church is the people of God, even as the nation of Israel was in the Old Testament. And Paul clearly understood that the moral exhortations to community holiness applied to Christian congregations.

But Paul's chief concern is not with the society outside the church, which, he says, God will judge. Paul is writing to the church about defaulting on their responsibility to take care of what goes on inside. Bruce Winter has observed, "The ease with which the present-day church often passes judgment on the ethical or structural misconduct of the outside community is at times matched only by its reluctance to take action to remedy the ethical conduct of its own members."[5] The church has a unique charge with the gospel and must act to protect its witness to it.

Implications for All Believers

At Capitol Hill Baptist Church, we exercise church disciple in some thought-out and well-defined areas. First, we excommunicate members for nonattendance. If someone attends regularly with no known, unrepentant sin, we consider them to be members in good standing. However, if we are aware of a member who is tolerating a particular sin in his (or her) life, we first work individually with the unrepentant one; then, if the member refuses to repent (see Matthew 18), we excommunicate him, praying all the while for his repentance.

We can follow those biblical guidelines with the members we know, but what of members whose lives we know nothing about? For their own sakes we cannot allow them to remain as members. All church members need to be regularly involved with others who can and will know them and serve them in this area of accountability. The chances for self-deception are just too great in all of us not to require accountability—something we see clearly from the man in 1 Corinthians 5. Part of our main business in glorifying God is by tending to such matters.

Another implication to consider from 1 Corinthians 5 is our culpability in someone else's sin. If we know of unrepentant sin in another member's life, but we do not follow the instructions for confrontation that Jesus laid out in Matthew 18, then we are actually acting as an accomplice in the sin. We are doing a disservice to them, to Christ, and to the world, which ought to be able to look at us and see that we are different, that tolerance is not the kindest thing.

According to Paul, how ought we to treat those whom we have excommunicated? A lot of particulars will shape the answer in each case, but in general we are to do what Paul said: "You must not associate with anyone who calls himself a brother but is sexually immoral. . . . With such a man do not even eat" (v. 11). Certainly that precludes spending casual time with the excommunicated one. Basically, we are not to act in any way that will cause him or her to think little of the church's action. We are not called to shun the person absolutely; for example, the one being disciplined is always welcome to come and attend the public worship of God, to hear his Word preached, and to be challenged and convicted by those means God has provided for his or her repentance.

Judging Those Who Are Inside

After addressing the particular sin situation in the Corinthian church, Paul now goes more deeply into the principles behind the call for believers to judge one another.

For Outsiders

First, we are to exercise godly judgment for the sake of outsiders. According to Paul, judging in this manner is part of our witness to those outside the church. Not only is judging our responsibility and our destiny and a service we offer to one another; it is part of our witness to the world. Paul writes:

> If any of you has a dispute with another, dare he take it before the ungodly for judgment instead of before the saints? Do you not know that the saints will judge the world? And if you are to judge the world, are you not competent to judge trivial cases? Do you not know that we will judge angels? How much more the things of this life! Therefore, if you have disputes about such matters, appoint as judges even men of little account in the church! I say this to shame you. Is it possible that there is nobody among you wise enough to judge a dispute between believers? But instead, one brother goes to law against another—and this in front of unbelievers! (6:1–6)

The Corinthian courts had a reputation for corruption. Judgments reflected the status of the litigants; verdicts were bought and sold. Therefore,

Christians taking their internal disputes to be settled in those courts was a monumental failure—not least in the witness they were providing to the non-Christians around them. That is why Paul does not want them seeking settlement by means of outsiders.

After all, Paul says, since Christians will eventually judge the entire world (v. 2), they certainly ought to contain their internal discrepancies among themselves. If we will judge angels (v. 3), we can certainly determine these things. Since believers will sit together with Christ judging all of creation, they can certainly handle today's minor disputes. (cf. 2 Pet. 2:4; Heb. 1:14; Jude 6). Paul stresses his point, noting that almost anyone in the church, even men of little account, should be able to adjudicate such disputes (1 Cor. 6:4–5). But the Corinthians were not seeking resolution from within their midst. They were taking their disputes before outsiders (v. 6).

We do not want to bring our petty disputes, which can so easily misrepresent the good news of Christ, to unbelievers; we want to bring them the gospel instead. We want them to see in us the hope for a life focused on more important things than on whatever can be gained in a secular court. That is why we must avoid suing one another. Christ is not divided, and we don't want to teach unbelievers the opposite by our comparatively petty divisions.

My friends, consider how your actions reflect the gospel. Be willing to give extra time in order to get involved in conflict resolution between your brothers and sisters. It is better for our primary mission that we keep that kind of work *inside* the church. All of us need to do this, helping each other with disputes in our marriages and families and among friends. This kind of judging is part of the work of the church for the sake of our witness to outsiders.

For Ourselves

Containing judgment within the church is also for our own benefit, the second reason Paul gives for his argument. He writes, "The very fact that you have lawsuits among you means you have been completely defeated already. Why not rather be wronged? Why not rather be cheated? Instead, you yourselves cheat and do wrong, and you do this to your brothers" (vv. 7–8).

Such internal judging can help to inculcate selfless love and humility. The very fact that we take offense shows a misunderstanding of what we deserve. We should want to act in humility toward each other and for the good of others. Avoiding lawsuits outside the church by taking care of any judging that needs to be done inside the church is consistent with this and should help to cultivate love and humility. According to Paul, lawsuits between church members revealed that the Corinthians had failed to understand that it is better to be wronged than to obscure their witness to outsiders. Their litigious actions showed the comprehensive failure of both the individuals involved and the Corinthian church as a whole. They were not content to be wronged, so they chose to wrong someone else.

We do not know exactly how they were cheating each other, but however they were doing it, the presence of lawsuits shows that they were in conflict, and that the conflicts had become public. We Christians want to show to the non-Christian public, more than anything else, a demonstration of Christ's selfless love and humility. We must learn that we cannot show that if we are squabbling over smaller matters ourselves.

My brothers and sisters, we claim to follow Christ, but which way did he go? He went the way of complete self-giving. Think again—do you really want to follow him? Listen to your soul. Do you find yourself feeling sharply the wrongs others have done to you? Do you remember the Lord's prayer, where we ask God to forgive us *as we have forgiven others*? What would need to change in your own heart for you to be more content to be wrongly treated? Judge within the church for your own sake.

For the Self-deceived

The third reason Paul gives for the need to judge within the church is for the sake of the self-deceived. Judging is actually kind. Oh, friends, be truthful about wickedness and its penalties in order to see people saved from it—as you have been! That is what Paul is saying here:

> Do you not know that the wicked will not inherit the kingdom of God? Do not be deceived: Neither the sexually immoral nor idolaters nor adulterers nor male prostitutes nor homosexual offenders nor thieves nor the greedy nor drunkards nor slanderers nor swindlers will inherit the kingdom of God. And that is what some of you were. But you were washed, you were sanctified, you were justified in the name of the Lord Jesus Christ and by the Spirit of our God. (vv. 9–11)

All the sins that Paul condemns here were common in ancient Corinth. But Paul is clear about the results. None of these—the sexually immoral, nor the idolaters, nor those whose lives are given to theft or swindling or any of these other things—will be saved if they continue such practices. Paul is not mandating perfect mastery over every sin as the price to enter heaven; God delights to justify the wicked (Rom. 4:5). What Paul is getting at is that the life of a truly regenerate person will not be marked by greed, slander, or any of these other sins. God saves Christians not only from the penalty of such sins but from the actual sins. We know from Romans 6 that newness of life is typical for the Christian; we have been born again. On the other hand, disobedience demonstrates unbelief (see John 3:36). Friends, the stakes in this are high. This is why nominal Christianity is such a danger. We are called in our churches to judge for the sake of the self-deceived.

We must all be careful of self-deception. The role of the church is to help other believers in exactly this. If you are a Christian, you are living in this fallen world differently from the way in which you would have been living otherwise. As John Newton stated one day in family prayers, "I am not what I ought to be. I am not what I wish to be. I am not what I hope to be. Yet I can truly say, I am not what I once was. *By the grace of God* I am what I am."

Paul reminds us here that Christ has saved those of us who are Christians from the kind of life he outlines here—"and this is what some of you *were*." We are saved by grace, and repentance is part of that, as is the continuing transforming work of the Holy Spirit. Even in something like the wonderfully grace-centered parable of the Prodigal Son in Luke 15, the son isn't simply forgiven—he returns. His life changes, and it is a wonderful thing that it does.

So for the sake of the self-deceived, we must lovingly judge. As Dietrich Bonhoeffer said, "Nothing can be more cruel than the tenderness that consigns another to his sin. Nothing can be more compassionate than the severe rebuke that calls a brother back from the path of sin. It is a ministry of mercy." So, beloved, repent of your sins. Remember—like John Newton—what God has done in your life, and don't be deceived. We in our congregations must pledge to do our best to help one another. We must welcome all, but we will love others so much that we will not love their sin. Instead we will be compassionately clear about sin. Judge within the church for the sake of the self-deceived.

For God

The fourth reason Paul gives for judging within the church is that we owe it to God.

"Everything is permissible for me"—but not everything is beneficial. "Everything is permissible for me"—but I will not be mastered by anything. "Food for the stomach and the stomach for food"—but God will destroy them both. The body is not meant for sexual immorality, but for the Lord, and the Lord for the body. By his power God raised the Lord from the dead, and he will raise us also. Do you not know that your bodies are members of Christ himself? Shall I then take the members of Christ and unite them with a prostitute? Never! Do you not know that he who unites himself with a prostitute is one with her in body? For it is said, "The two will become one flesh." But he who unites himself with the Lord is one with him in spirit. Flee from sexual immorality. All other sins a man commits are outside his body, but he who sins sexually sins against his own body. Do you not know that your body is a temple of the Holy Spirit, who is in you, whom you have received from God? You are not your own; you were bought at a price. Therefore honor God with your body. (6:12–20)

To commit sexual sin is to sin against our own bodies, but that is not the climax of Paul's argument; it is just a link in the chain to his point that our bodies belong to God. In other words, we owe it to God to judge each other about sexual sin because God cares what we do with our bodies—they are his.

In verses 12 and 13 Paul is apparently quoting some of the popular but false slogans that were circulating at the time: "Everything is permissible for me," and "food for the stomach and the stomach for food." Paul responds to these, saying that any casualness about physical conduct and physical sin is inappropriate because God will raise us physically, even as he did Christ (v. 14). Indifference to sexual activity because it is "only physical" is wrong. Since our bodies belong to God, we are not to use them for immorality (6:15). Besides, prostitution clearly opposes God's institution of marriage (6:16; Gen. 2:24).

Furthermore, we Christians have been spiritually joined to God (6:17) through believing and by the indwelling of God's Spirit. God's Holy Spirit resides in the Christian; he takes our bodies as his temple (see 3:16). Therefore, we must honor God with our bodies because we have been bought at a price. We are his by creation and by redemption.

We do not glorify God with our bodies by burnishing and polishing them at the gym until they shine; rather, we glorify him by using our bodies relationally and sexually in the ways God has instructed us in his Word. Paul stressed these physical sins because they were an area of particularly and perversely proud disinterest to the "spiritual" party in Corinth. We know from elsewhere in the New Testament that doctrinal error and love-less divisiveness are grounds for the church to judge someone within their number. But here in chapters 5 and 6 it is particularly immorality that we see as a cause for such judging.

Friend, God cares about what you do with your body. Caring for physical life and a moral and right use of the body honors God. This is doubly true if you are a Christian because you are following Christ, your resurrected Lord, because you too will be raised. Beloved, consider how blessed you are—intimately united to God, indwelt by his Spirit, bought with the price of his only begotten Son. We are people treasured by God. If we as a church are to follow Christ, we must work to teach and model and inculcate correct relations between people sexually and socially because doing so honors God. We judge within the church for God's sake.

Conclusion

The set of people who comprise the local church are centered on Jesus Christ; they are also bounded by a visible commitment to following him. Sin is and will be in the life of every believer in the church. Unrepentant sin must cease. Struggled against—yes; discouraging from season to season—it will happen; shaming and harming us—even that is so. But ruling us so that it typifies us and we are therefore rightly characterized and summed up by it as these examples in Corinth show us—no. One aspect of the love of God is hatred of sin.

William Arnot was a minister in the Free Church of Scotland in the middle of the nineteenth century. Among other useful work, he left a wonderful commentary on the book of Proverbs. At one point in that commentary, he writes this passage that I think challenges us well about the concern we in the church should have about sin:

> Its theme throughout is righteousness, the fruit of faith. We who live under the Christian dispensation should beware of a fatal mistake in our conception of its distinguishing characteristic. The gospel is not a method of bringing men to heaven without righteousness, or with less of it than was demanded in ancient times. The actual holiness of his creatures is the end of the Lord in all his dispensations, as certainly as fruit is the object of the husbandman when he plants, and waters, and grafts his trees. The death of Christ for sin is the divine plan, not for dispensing with obedience from men, but for effectu-ally obtaining it. Reconciliation is the road to righteousness. God proclaims

pardon and bestows peace, that the rebels may submit and serve him. They who feel more at ease in their alienation because they have heard that Christ gave himself for sinners, are trampling under foot the blood of the covenant. Alas! Even God's dear Son is made the stumbling-block over which men fall blindfold. A vague impression comes in and possesses a corrupt heart, that personal holiness is in some way less needful under the reign of grace. God is my witness, I have not . . . taught that men should try their own obedience, instead of trusting in the Saviour for the free pardon of sin: but I have taught often, and once more tenderly repeat the lesson here, that those who do not like the obligation to obedience, have no part yet in the forgiving grace.

The whole world consists of two classes, different in many things from each other but alike in this, that both are obliged to labour all their days: they are those who serve sin, and those who fight against it. Both experience pain and weariness; sin is a hard master, and a formidable foe. If you do its bidding, you are a miserable drudge; if you war against it, you will receive many wounds in the conflict. It would be hard to tell whether of the two is the more wearied—the carnal who obeys the flesh, or the spiritual who crucifies it. Both are compelled to labour. Both are weary: the one is weary by sinning, and the other weary of sin. One of these strifes will soon be over: the other will never cease. If sin be your antagonist, there will soon be peace; for if sin cannot be taken wholly away from you, you will ere long be taken away from sin. But if sin be, and till death abide, your master, there is no deliverance from the yoke.[6]

By God's grace our churches will oppose sin's cruel ways in people's lives. To neglect to discipline sinners is to neglect our proper business, to act to ruin the church for which Christ died, and to harm the person caught in such sin. To refuse to judge sin in the church is to obscure the gospel, harm ourselves, especially the weakest and most vulnerable among us—those trapped in their sins—and to dishonor God himself. It has been said, and truly, that when discipline leaves a church, Christ goes with it. Let us pray that Christ will never desert this church, and that we will never desert him.

5

ASCETICISM

1 CORINTHIANS 7

I once initiated a conversation with someone in the Albany airport. He was tall; he had a long beard, a black hat, and distinctively clerical, black robes reaching all the way to the floor. Needless to say, he was a striking contrast to those of us from our church staff who were lounging at the airport gate casually dressed, reading our newspapers, and checking our e-mail. The man in the airport had a little book written in Cyrillic script that he was reading intently.

I introduced myself to him, telling him that all the guys sitting around him were Baptist pastors, and that we were curious what he was reading. He told me, and with that we began a long and interesting conversation. I told him my name. He then introduced himself as "Seraphim." Taken a little aback, I asked him (before I could self-edit) "You mean like in 'and cherubim'?" He smiled and said yes.

Seraphim is a Greek Orthodox monk. As we continued to talk, he told me that he was on a quest for a life in which anger, lust, and greed are no more. By becoming a monk, he had set out to pursue a higher plane of spiritual experience, one that would subdue all feelings. He wanted a spiritual experience in which all of the passions were completely transcended. That's why monks sequester themselves from the world, he explained. That's why they foreswear marriage and other worldly occupations, and give themselves to Bible reading, prayer, and study. The pleasures of this world are, for Seraphim, clearly something not to be trusted. He talked as excitedly of Anthony's experiences from the Egyptian desert in the fourth century as if Anthony was all over the front page of today's newspapers. Seraphim was a comparatively rare example today of someone who gives himself over to asceticism in the name of Christ.

Most people today go in the opposite direction. We tend to think that worldly circumstances are all-important, and when we think this way, we naturally conclude that the problems we have will be solved by simply changing our circumstances. In this we are a bit like Seraphim. We think of our marital status and our employment as the all-important aspects of our lives, the things that shape and determine our goodness, happiness, satisfaction, and general usefulness to God. And today, when these areas of our lives are not going well, we don't seek to renounce them; we seek to change them. We think the answers lie in having *different* worldly circumstances. So we confidently, restlessly, maybe even desperately act to change our situation. We seek a new job, a new social status, a spouse, or, if we already have one, a different spouse.

Getting Serious

Today's way of looking at the world isn't new. It has been around for a long time. It was around in the first century, when Paul wrote to the church in Corinth. First Corinthians 7 addresses exactly this sort of mind-set. There is so much we could consider from this chapter. We certainly won't be able to cover everything, but I doubt we will have much motivation to study any of it *if* we don't first sort through one of the questions people most often have when they read this chapter: given what we read in some of the verses, specifically, 1 Corinthians 7:10, 12, 25, and 40, are Paul's words here inspired? The short answer is yes, they are inspired.

In verse 10 Paul writes, "To the married I give this command (not I, but the Lord): A wife must not separate from her husband." Paul understands his instructions to approximate Christ's prohibition of divorce, which is why he says that this is something Jesus said. Then in verse 12 Paul writes, "To the rest I say this (I, not the Lord): If any brother has a wife who is not a believer and she is willing to live with him, he must not divorce her." Here Paul is simply continuing to answer their questions, but he is now doing so without referencing any particular teaching of Jesus. This is what he is doing again in verse 25: "Now about virgins: I have no command from the Lord, but I give a judgment as one who by the Lord's mercy is trustworthy." Verse 40 is also debated: "In my judgment, she is happier if she stays as she is—and I think that I too have the Spirit of God." Here Paul is asserting his dependability, not over against Jesus but over against the false teachers mentioned in the first four chapters of the epistle.

Paul *knew* the teaching of Christ, and he did not want to succumb to any temptation to create new teachings in Christ's name. This was all way too serious and important, and the first generation of Christians in particular took care to preserve the words of Jesus. Paul resisted any temptation to create words, regardless of how convenient it would have been to have done so in dealing with the Corinthians here.

The other thing I think we need to consider is this: are Paul's words simply advice—even inspired advice—for a situation that no longer applies to Christians today? Paul refers to "the present crisis" in verse 26. What is the *present crisis* Paul refers to there? Basically, this crisis, or as Don Carson prefers to translate it, this "compulsion," is the situation in which Christians find themselves between the resurrection and Christ's return. We are told that there is to be increasing tribulation as the end of the age nears (see Luke 21:23); therefore, whatever Paul may have been referring to in the immediate context of the Corinthian church would simply amplify the Corinthians' already-existing "present crisis."

Some commentators have suggested that Paul was referring specifically to alarming circumstances present in Corinth at the time. Food shortages and famines have been written about, as well as earthquakes, and when you remember that Jesus said that earthquakes and famines were to precede the end, you can see how the Corinthians might have been especially excited that perhaps the end was near. Furthermore, any sort of religious persecution threatening them would simply heighten their need to live with the end in view.

We find the same pattern of expression in verse 29 where Paul writes, "The time is short." Calvin said that this is simply a reference to the brevity of life (as are so many other references in Scripture; e.g., James 4:14; 1 Pet. 1:24). But for the Christian, time has been foreshortened, as it were, as knowledge of the future has been brought into the present. For us as Christians, the future has appeared. The last days began with the resurrection of Jesus Christ, the firstfruit from among the dead. Christians have a different perspective. We live with the light of the future streaming back into the present, which effectually rearranges our priorities in the here and now. We know that Christ is returning and that this world is passing away (cf. 1 Cor. 1:7–8; Rom. 13:11–12; Luke 14:26). The future has become clear; it is plain to us, and that affects how we live. So I think that while the debated phrases Paul used may indicate some special urgency in the Corinthians' lives, basically he was addressing them from the same vantage point at which we Christians find ourselves today.

Now that we have addressed some of the issues that might impede our study of 1 Corinthians 7, we can get to the heart of Paul's teaching here with three simple points. The first two points concern marriage; the third point addresses our personal circumstances.

Marry, and Stay Married

In the first sixteen verses of chapter 7, Paul writes about marriage. In fact, this chapter is the most direct, extended teaching on marriage in the Bible. What we see here is that marriage is good—Paul tells people to get married and to stay married.

The chapter begins with a contrary teaching. Paul writes, "Now for the matters you wrote about: It is good for a man not to marry," or more literally, as other translations render it, "it is good for a man not to touch a woman." Is Paul teaching here that it is good for a man not to touch a woman, or is Paul addressing an error that has crept into the Corinthian church? When we look closely at his words, it is apparent that the latter is in view. Paul was responding to a distorted teaching that to "touch a woman," a euphemism for sexual intimacy, was perhaps not very spiritual, which then threw into question the whole concept of marriage.

Corinth—like other ancient port cities—was a morally confusing place for the members of a young church existing in its midst. A husband or wife might be converted to Christ while his or her spouse was not. Did this invalidate the marriage? Another question arose upon the death of a spouse. Should the surviving one remarry? And what about divorce? Into the midst of such complexities came false teachers who offered asceticism as the answer to such questions. That is the context for Paul's discussion in chapter 7.

One of Paul's primary concerns was to prevent immorality, so he instructs each man to have his own wife and each woman her own husband. Paul affirms marriage, in no small part because singleness is so dangerous sexually and therefore spiritually. Paul clearly separates himself from the ascetics as he continues: "The husband should fulfill his marital duty to his wife, and likewise the wife to her husband" (v. 3). He exhorts the married to have sexual relations, perhaps because the believers in Corinth were (wrongly) denying it to their non-Christian spouses. Whatever the situation, Paul makes clear that those who marry give their bodies to one another. The husband owns the wife's body, and the wife is said to own the husband's body, a unique statement in the context of the ancient world that shows something of the esteem and respect with which Christians treated women. This mutual owning shows us that the sexual relationship in marriage is a way to give love. Our greatest satisfaction—even sexually—will normally come in bringing satisfaction to our spouse.

The giving nature of the sexual union as designed by God is one reason that rape and other sexual abuses are so terrible. They are grotesque caricatures of marriage. A physical relationship, meant to be joyful and satisfying and encouraging, instead becomes the reason for sadness and despair, all because of a diabolical and tragic self-centeredness on the part of the rapist or the abuser.

But because the sexual aspect of marriage is so important, Paul stresses that abstinence from it must be only for limited times and specific purposes: "Do not deprive each other except by mutual consent and for a time, so that you may devote yourselves to prayer. Then come together again so that Satan will not tempt you because of your lack of self-control. I say this as a concession, not as a command" (vv. 5–6). Paul is not giving reluctant concession to the enjoyment of sex; it is the abstinence he concedes to.

Those who do not know the Bible well are often surprised to learn that God is pro-sex. After all, he designed and created it. Marriage is a good gift of God's, not just to Christians but to all people. In theological terms, marriage is a creation ordinance, meaning that it is rooted not in the life of the church (unlike baptism and the Lord's Supper) but in the life of the world by God's design at creation. God designed marriage to be enjoyed by all races, classes, religions, and ethnicities.

Marital sex has been given to us for many reasons. We see in the first few chapters of Genesis that marriage is for partnership and procreation. We also find that it points to our lack of self-sufficiency (Genesis 2). Another reason sex has been given is for protection, a truth we see here in 1 Corinthians 7 and also in the book of Proverbs. Sex has been given also for pleasure. Another purpose for sex is the public good (Prov. 6:20–35). Additionally, sex is a reflection of God's relationship with his people and Christ's with his church, as we see from the Old Testament prophets and in Ephesians 5.

If we use sex solely for pleasure, we miss out on partnership, procreation, contributing to the public good, and participating in true intimacy. If we misuse sex, we end up trashing one of God's sweet gifts to us. We also sin against God. My friend, if your life has been characterized by sexual sin, you need forgiveness and a reconciled relationship with God, and that can be found only through Christ.

Paul continues on the topic of marriage for several more verses, teaching that God gifts people differently in the area of marriage. He writes, "I wish that all men were as I am. But each man has his own gift from God; one has this gift, another has that" (v. 7). Both marriage and singleness are God's gifts through his Spirit for the building up of his church (cf. Matt. 19:12). Paul indicates here and in verse 8 that it is good for the unmarried to remain unmarried. Along the same lines, Paul tells the Corinthians that unless they were compelled to do otherwise, they were to stay in their marriages (vv. 9–16). In verse 10, Paul alludes to Christ's teaching against divorce as a way of undermining any anti-marriage teaching that would justify dissolving existing marriages. Believers should stay married to their non-Christian spouses; verse 14 makes clear that God regards such marriages as legitimate, with the implication that the offspring of these marriages are legitimate as well. According to verse 15 believers can remarry if they are deserted by their non-Christian spouse. But believers in turn are not to abandon an unbelieving spouse because remaining might just lead to the salvation of the unbeliever (v. 16).

If you are married, the Lord's basic instruction to you is to stay married, and part of doing so is to have sex. Sex is not only good; it is an important part of marriage. You have no right to take your body away from your spouse, any more than you have a right to take your own life. God has joined you to your spouse; you *belong* to your spouse.

If you are a divorced Christian, your first duty in regard to marriage is to be reconciled to your spouse. If, however, you have been deserted, Paul clearly teaches that you can accept that divorce; you are no longer bound and are free to remarry.

Because marriage is so important, so valuable, churches do well to offer premarital counseling and to perform weddings and to hold small groups for young married couples. Because marriage is so important, churches must discipline any member who proceeds with an unbiblical divorce. And because marriage is so important, churches must recognize some divorces as legitimate and be willing to perform weddings for some being remarried. Marry, and stay married!

Some Should Not Marry

The next portion of chapter 7 (vv. 25–40), makes clear that there are some who should not marry.

Before we examine these verses, let me give you a word on the mind-set that was common in Greek culture. The immaterial soul was thought of as valuable, but the material body was considered relatively unimportant. That is why it was so scandalous for Paul to preach the bodily resurrection in Athens and among Greeks elsewhere. The resurrection of the body was viewed among some as unnecessary and grotesque and even ridiculous. This mind/body dualism led to one of two responses. Some became stoic and ascetic, denying their bodily requirements. Others went the opposite direction and became Epicureans, feeding their bodily desires, assuming that physical indulgences were of no significance or consequence. This was the mind-set of many, and it was in this context—belittling the importance of the physical—that strange teachings had come up in the Corinthian congregation.

This whole section of the epistle (7:25–40) pertains to the sexually inexperienced. Paul knew of no teaching from Jesus on this matter, as he states in verse 25. But apparently he had been asked about it, so he sent them an answer. How were the sexually inexperienced supposed to live as Christians? To the single folks, Paul was essentially saying, at least to some of them, "Don't get married."

There are some who say that the only people who are called to singleness are those who have no sexual desires, but that is not quite what Paul seems to be saying here. Though there are people who have no sexual desire, or extremely low levels of it, Paul has already mentioned (v. 9) that many single people do have such desires that must be controlled. Sexual desires alone are not a sufficient call to marriage.

There are a number of reasons Paul lays out here for some to not marry. First, he mentions the exigencies of life in this world: "Because of the present crisis, I think that it is good for you to remain as you are" (v. 26). There may be reference here to some specific difficulties of the time, difficulties that could be handled more easily without a spouse.

Second, Paul says that although marriage is certainly not sin, it *is* troublesome (v. 28). Of course, having a family necessitates agonizing choices. Many single people feel mightily afflicted by their single status, but the troubles of singleness may be exceeded by the difficulties encountered in marriage.

Third, Paul argues that believers are free to pass on marriage because marriage is *part of this world that is passing away* (vv. 29–31). "What I mean, brothers, is that the time is short. From now on those who have wives should live as if they had none; those who mourn, as if they did not; those who are happy, as if they were not; those who buy something, as if it were not theirs to keep; those who use the things of the world, as if not engrossed in them. For this world in its present form is passing away." So all these classes of people should live keeping in mind the impermanence of things in this life.

If you are not a believer, do take to heart Paul's warning here that the time is short. This world is passing away. Do you understand what we Christians mean by that? For those of us who believe and are aware of the brevity of life, the subject makes for a great conversation to have with our friends.

A fourth reason to remain unmarried, Paul warns the sexually inexperienced in the Corinthian congregation, is the *preoccupations* that marriage entails. In verse 32 Paul explains that an unmarried man is free to devote himself to the Lord, while a married man (v. 33) must concern himself with pleasing his wife. And then he says the same thing for the women in verse 34. There is good teaching about marriage here, even though this portion of the letter focuses on singleness. Paul's primary desire is that singles live in undivided devotion to the Lord: "I am saying this for your own good, not to restrict you, but that you may live in a right way in undivided devotion to the Lord" (v. 35).

So in all of this does Paul really sound any different than my monk friend? Is Paul advocating asceticism here? He is not. Paul is teaching the need for moderation and for a heavenly perspective on this world. Paul cannot be classed as an ascetic if for no other reason than what he said in verse 3, where he specifically enjoined sexual relations as a duty between a husband and his wife. Any preference Paul has for singleness is not rooted in a desire to deny pleasure but rather to encourage God-centeredness.

Paul continues, instructing the Corinthian believers that they are free to do as they want in regard to marrying:

> If anyone thinks he is acting improperly toward the virgin he is engaged to, and if she is getting along in years and he feels he ought to marry, he should do as he wants. He is not sinning. They should get married. But the man who has settled the matter in his own mind, who is under no compulsion but has control over his own will, and who has made up his mind not to marry the

virgin—this man also does the right thing. So then, he who marries the virgin does right, but he who does not marry her does even better. (vv. 36–38)

What the New International Version (NIV) translates as "the virgin he is engaged to," the original Greek renders as "his virgin." The NIV along with the New Revised Standard Version (NRSV) and the English Standard Version (ESV) have taken this to be addressing a man and his fiancée. The New American Standard Bible (NASB) has taken this to be referring to a man and his daughter. The older translations such as Tyndale and the King James Version simply leave it ambiguous— "his virgin." Whichever it may actually be, Paul is telling the Corinthians that proceeding with marriage was not necessarily sinful. Perhaps under the influence of some false, ascetical teaching some of the fathers had pledged their daughters to virginity, and Paul is saying that it is okay to release them from those vows. But, on the other hand, continued virginity is also not sinful; in fact, Paul has been arguing throughout this section its advantages. Paul concludes the chapter in verses 39 and 40 by advising widows that they would do better not to remarry, although they can be married again to a Christian if they wish.

Throughout this section, Paul has argued that singleness is better than marriage for some Christians—including himself. Basically, Paul seems to be saying to single people in the Corinthian congregation that if they are sexually controlled and spiritually motivated for singleness, then they may consider themselves to be gifted for singleness. On the other hand, they may still decide for spiritual motivations to get married. However, he makes clear that single Christians are free to decide that they are an exception to the general principles set forth in Genesis 2:18—"The LORD God said, 'It is not good for the man to be alone'"—and in 1 Corinthians 7:2—"Since there is so much immorality, each man should have his own wife, and each woman her own husband." A decision for or away from marriage is serious, and is best not taken lightly or alone. Singles do well to seek counsel about the wisdom of remaining single, but it is the right decision for some.

I hope you were struck by Paul's words, "An unmarried man is concerned about the Lord's affairs—how he can please the Lord" (v. 32). When I pondered that, I thought, really? Is that *really* the case? Of course, what Paul is saying here is that people unencumbered by marriage and family are able to be so concerned. To my single brothers and sisters I would simply ask you if such a concern about the Lord's affairs marks you, or do you think, "When I find a spouse, then I will serve the Lord"? Whether you are committed to being unmarried or would love to marry tomorrow, your singleness today comes from the providential hand of God. Are you using it well? If you are desirous of a spouse, how are you influenced by your concern for the Lord's affairs on what kind of a person you are looking for in a spouse? You can be sure that a biblically based congregation will never allow any of its single members to knowingly marry a non-Christian.

In my congregation we mean to honor singleness. We want to help our members think about using their singleness well. While we don't believe it is a superior calling (as some have said), we also don't believe it is an inferior calling to marriage. Two of our elders are unmarried men. Singleness was the calling of Paul and of Christ himself, who was in no way imperfectly human. Some, Paul says, should not marry at all.

Our Present Circumstances

The third point I want to highlight from 1 Corinthians 7 is that our circumstances in the here and now are not ultimate. This is the primary point Paul is making in verses 17 to 24. The lesson is an important one for the Corinthians because outward circumstances carried significant weight in Corinth. Jews were tolerated but looked down upon and sometimes persecuted. Jews regarded Gentiles as unclean. A large segment of the population was enslaved to a small part of the population. As in our own day, economic and ethnic and religious differences seriously affected the lives of the Corinthians, which was why Paul saw the importance of minimizing their earthly lot.

Our chief concern is not to be our circumstances here and now, and an awareness of this helps us use what we have here and now correctly. Our confidence is that this world is passing, and another is coming. Such confidence is not to make us desperate to change our circumstances nor indifferent to our earthly lot. Rather, such confidence should free us to engage more fully in our circumstances, realizing that they are neither permanent or ultimate.

We have not been created for the purpose of finding our ultimate satisfaction in a job. There is no spouse whom we were ever meant to take as the ultimate concern of our life. We have been made for the purpose of knowing God.

Each one should retain the place in life that the Lord assigned to him and to which God has called him. This is the rule I lay down in all the churches. Was a man already circumcised when he was called? He should not become uncircumcised. Was a man uncircumcised when he was called? He should not be circumcised. Circumcision is nothing and uncircumcision is nothing. Keeping God's commands is what counts. Each one should remain in the situation which he was in when God called him. Were you a slave when you were called? Don't let it trouble you—although if you can gain your freedom, do so. For he who was a slave when he was called by the Lord is the Lord's freedman; similarly, he who was a free man when he was called is Christ's slave. You were bought at a price; do not become slaves of men. Brothers, each man, as responsible to God, should remain in the situation God called him to. (vv. 17–24)

The general principle Paul is setting forth in this passage is that the Corinthians were to remain in the state in which they found themselves when God called them to salvation. According to verse 17, the rule Paul gives for believers everywhere and in every age is that their calling to God is primary, whatever their situation in life.

In verses 18 and 19 Paul illustrates this by teaching about circumcision, the mark of Jewish identity. Paul says that obedience is more important than circumcision. Paul sums up the circumcision issue by reiterating his main principle in this section—the Corinthian believers are to understand their call to God as the primary issue (v. 20).

In verses 21 to 24 Paul brings out a second illustration of the principle that our circumstances here and now are not ultimate. Addressing Christians who are slaves (v. 21), Paul says that they should remain in their slavery, not being overly concerned to gain their freedom but certainly taking hold of freedom if doing so is possible. In first-century Corinth, slavery was not racial, nor strictly chattel, slavery. Many if not most of the slaves had rights; they were essentially in an economic contract with their masters. It was not uncommon for people to sell themselves into slavery for the advantages that could be gained and then to buy themselves out some years later. Teachers, doctors, and accountants were often slaves, along with household servants, table waiters, and other manual laborers.

When Paul writes, "He who was a slave when he was called by the Lord is the Lord's freedman; similarly, he who was a free man when he was called is Christ's slave" (v. 22), he is saying that our relationship to God is most important. No matter our calling, we are his freedmen and his bondservants through Christ. There is both a liberation and a servitude that all Christians share. All this does not mean that earthly circumstances are completely unimportant, which is why Paul advises the Corinthians that they should avoid becoming enslaved. However, as Paul sums up in verse 24, we are to understand our calling to God as the most important thing, regardless of our situation in life. As Bruce Winter puts it, "The covetous, driven search for mobility was prohibited."[1]

Paul is not advocating slavery, as is clear from his words in verse 21 that encourage a slave to obtain freedom if the opportunity arises. His words in verse 21, taken together with his words in verse 23 forbidding one from entering voluntarily into slavery and his statement elsewhere forbidding slave trading (1 Tim. 1:10), effectively prohibit Christians from promoting slavery. But *challenging* slavery in the general social, economic, and political structures of the Roman Empire was not to be the Christian's immediate goal or duty. One can live as a Christian slave (see Eph. 6:5–8; Col. 3:23; 1 Tim. 6:1–2), although living as a Christian slave owner is contradictory. Paul's instruction to slaves here in Corinthians is similar to his instructions about marriage—an unequally yoked marriage should not be contracted, but it should be honored if it has occurred. The primary disconnect between the two is that marriage is a creation ordinance whereas slavery is a distortion of a creation ordinance regarding work.

All that having been said, Paul is clear that our circumstances are not to be viewed as ultimate. He summarizes his point in verses 29 to 31:

> What I mean, brothers, is that the time is short. From now on those who have wives should live [be] as if they had none; those who mourn, as if they did not; those who are happy, as if they were not; those who buy something, as if it were not theirs to keep; those who use the things of the world, as if not engrossed in them. For this world in its present form is passing away.

Richard Sibbes preached on these verses calling his sermon, "The Spiritual Man's Aim: Guiding a Christian in his affections and actions through the sundry passages of this life. So that God's glory, and his own salvation may be the main end of all."[2] The uncertainty of the world should take our hearts from the love of it. Heavenly matters are never to be secondary.

My Christian brother or sister, stop focusing on your worldly circumstances. Of course, our non-Christian friends may define themselves completely by such circumstances, but that's because they think that is all there is. But you know better! Resist the urge to conform to the world by caring most about these things. I wonder what circumstances you might be in that you cannot press into the service of Christ and God's glory? Submit everything to God, my brothers and sisters.

The power of passing circumstances is diminished by the fact that we, as believers, do not share all worldly circumstances in common. Jesus is best displayed by the differences that exist between us—marriage and singleness, Jew and Gentile, rich and poor, manual laborer and capitalist, old and young, male and female, black and white, Asian and African, from all parts of the country, with children and without, struggling and confident. What do we all have in common? Only Jesus. Diversity in our circumstances glorifies God and his gospel because we have Christ and his gospel in common. We want to be a community that lives in contradiction to the common agenda of structuring life around worldly attributes and goals. A homogeneous congregation would undermine the universality of the very message that we are seeking to set forth.

Our circumstances here and now are not ultimate. Paul knew it; he lived it, and he called the Corinthians to live it too. Likewise God calls us to show it in our lives and in our congregations.

Conclusion

Asceticism is not a healthy, biblical option for us as Christians or for us to teach to our congregations. We are to relativize the importance of this world by keeping in mind the next and having our hearts set on the joy to be given us when Christ is revealed. We are to be marked not by a hatred of the physical but by a rigorous disciplining of it. We are not to live by denying the goodness of creation but by being willing to embrace what we lack for ends and goals that aren't limited.

Leo Tolstoy didn't write only long novels like *War and Peace*. He also wrote short stories. One of his stories is entitled, "How Much Land Does a Man Need?" and it is the story of a Russian, Pahom, and his family. Pahom is tempted through a conversation to discontentment with some of his worldly circumstances. The devil decides to give him land enough, and it is on that last word that the story hangs. Pahom goes through great toil and struggle to move his family in order to buy some land. Then, becoming discontent with the land, he repeats the process. The cycle of work, attainment, and discontent continues.

Finally, one day he hears of a tribe that is selling land in a most unusual way. The tribal chief tells Pahom that the tribe will sell him land at the price of a thousand rubles a day. When Pahom asks for an explanation of these terms, the chief explained that for one thousand rubles a man could get land by covering as much ground as possible between sunrise and sunset. All the covered ground would be his so long as he returned to his starting point before the sun went down. Pahom was delighted and could barely sleep the night before, as he anticipated all of the hundreds of acres he was about to own.

The next morning Pahom set out early and covered much ground. He included this bit of land and that bit as he walked on, urging himself along with the knowledge that the faster he moved, the more land he would have. But as the day wore on, Pahom wore out. Yet his appetite for more land in no way decreased. With every fiber of his being he worked to get every inch of land that he possibly could. He finally reached the place from which he had begun just as the sun was setting. The tribe gathered round him cheered as Pahom fell forward toward the chief. "Ah, that's a fine fellow!" exclaimed the chief. "He has gained much land!"

Just then Pahom's servant came running up to Pahom and tried to raise him, but he found that Pahom was dead! The tribe members clicked their tongues to show their pity. His servant picked up the spade and dug a grave long enough for Pahom to lie in and buried him in it. Six feet from his head to his heels was all the land he needed.

Oh, my friend, don't be like Pahom! Don't live as if this world and its circumstances are the point of life, the key to happiness. Live instead like B. B. Warfield whose wife was struck by lightning on their honeymoon, and who, for decades thereafter, was never away from her for more than a few hours at a time. Or be like Granny Brand, mother of British physician and Christian author Paul Brand. Granny Brand left prosperous prospects in London and gave her life as a missionary in a remote part of India. Some years after her death, her son Paul, himself a renowned doctor and a Christian author, was taken back by a friend to visit the place of his parents' labors decades earlier, which had been his childhood home in the Kolli Malai Mountains. One friend described his visit like this:

Suddenly the Jeep crested a small hill and an amazing sight met us. A hundred and fifty people were waiting alongside the road and had been waiting, we soon learned, for four hours. They surrounded our car, greeting us in the traditional Indian fashion, palms held together, head bowed. Women, colorful as tropical birds in their bright silk saris, draped floral leis around our necks and led us to a feast spread on banana leaves. After the meal everyone crowded into the mud-walled chapel built by Paul Brand's father and treated us to an hour-long program of hymns, tributes, and ceremonial dances. I remember one speech especially, by a woman who spoke of Paul's mother. "The hill tribes didn't practice abortion," she said. "They disposed of unwanted children by leaving them beside the road. Granny Brand would take in these children, nurse them back to health, rear them, and try to educate them. I was one of the unwanted ones, left to die. There were several dozen of us. . . . We called her Mother of the Hills. When I did well in studies, she paid for me to go off to a proper school, and eventually I earned a master's degree. I now teach nursing at the University of Madras, and I came several hundred miles today to honor the Brands for what they did for me and many others."[3]

Can you conceive of Granny Brand's own welcome in heaven? Don't live a life cramped by misunderstanding that your earthly circumstances are why you are alive. You are alive for something much bigger and much better than that—you are alive for God.

> From every tribe doth music rise, all nations form the choir;
> Ten thousand times that man were blest that might this music hear.

6

DISOBEDIENCE

1 CORINTHIANS 8:1–10:13

Hugh and Nicholas were both born in England. Hugh was about fifteen years older than Nicholas. He grew up on a farm in the middle of England (near Leicester) and went to Cambridge to study. He was hired to teach there and stayed on for a few years. Then, feeling called into the ministry, he became a preacher. Only afterward did Hugh come to hear and believe the gospel. One day, the king heard him preach and liked him, so Hugh was given a church to pastor off in the west country of England. He was a popular preacher—direct, empathetic, and witty.

Nicholas was born up near the Scottish border, and as he grew he also was sent south to Cambridge to study. Like Hugh before him, Nicholas did well (probably even better than Hugh), and eventually he too was hired as a teacher in Cambridge.

For a few years Hugh did really well. The king liked him so much that he made him one of his chaplains. He even made Hugh a bishop! At the same time, Nicholas became chaplain to another bishop and the head of one of the colleges at Cambridge.

But in middle age, Hugh fell into disfavor with the king. The king did not like some of the things Hugh said, and he didn't like some of the things that Hugh refused to do. At the same time, Nicholas was keeping his head down as the old king, Henry VIII, kept swerving back and forth between supporting and opposing the Protestant Reformation. Despite different backgrounds, both Hugh and Nicholas had become uncomfortably close to the tumultuous center of the changes going on in England.

Then the old king died, and his young son came to the throne. Hugh, who had by this time been imprisoned, was released and again became a popular preacher. Nicholas was made a bishop, and he helped to organize more biblically based church services. He became a champion for laying down personal freedoms in order to avoid divisiveness among Christians, especially when it came to simple things such as what ministers should wear.

Throughout their different lives and careers both Hugh and Nicholas had to learn to follow Christ and to obey him in a world that was always shifting and changing, a world in which right and wrong were hotly debated. In the last few years of their lives, both men determined to obey Christ in very difficult ways. They understood God's Word, and they had seen the examples of others around them—some good, some not so good.

I want to stop the story right there and go back to our study in 1 Corinthians. We turn now to consider some chapters in Paul's epistle pertaining to obedience—what obedience looks like and how we discern it—in situations similar to those that Hugh and Nicholas faced and in those that you and I face today. We want to look at a lengthy passage in the middle of Paul's epistle, 1 Corinthians 8:1–10:13. What we find here are three ways to learn obedience.

Obedience and Good Teaching

The first way we learn obedience is by means of good teaching, and we find the connection between them in 1 Corinthians 8. The topic Paul is addressing is food that had been sacrificed to idols. It was a hot topic!

Animal sacrifices were a regular part of ancient pagan worship. Slaughterhouses, where meat was often purchased, stood next to the temples. The meat sold at the slaughterhouses came from the sacrifices offered there. As a result, people prepared and served meat that had originated as a sacrifice in the neighborhood pagan temple. At the time of the animal sacrifice, some of the meat was burned; another portion often went to the temple staff. Other portions of the slaughtered animal were returned to the one offering the sacrifice or put up for sale in the slaughterhouse. The temple served as not only a place of worship but also as a butcher shop.

Anyone eating such meat might be considered a worshiper of the deity to which the sacrifice had been made, whether Artemis or Hermes or Apollo. Anyone who resolved to refrain from eating meat sacrificed to idols barred himself from participation in the public issues of the city as well as from local festivals and was hindered from rubbing shoulders with fellow citizens. This is the background to Paul's words here in chapter 8, where he instructed the Corinthian Christians about knowledge and about love.

The Truth about Knowledge

The Christians at Corinth knew that there is only one true God, but Paul is concerned that they did not understand the implications of this knowledge, so he writes, "Now about food sacrificed to idols: We know that we all possess knowledge. Knowledge puffs up, but love builds up. The man who thinks he knows something does not yet know as he ought to know. But the man who loves God is known by God" (1 Cor. 8:1–3). The knowledge Paul refers to here in 8:1 is the knowledge that there is one true God, regardless of the deity to which the sacrifices were made. Therefore, the believers in Corinth were free to eat meat sacrificed to idols.

But Paul cautions them that knowledge should be regulated by love. Perhaps those in the Corinthian church who prided themselves on being in the know weren't really as knowledgeable as they thought. Scripture is certainly the right source for our knowledge, but Paul here is also concerned that they learn and exercise their knowledge in the right context—the church.

There is a difference, with knowing, between exercising our rights and acting in love. So Paul challenges them to realize that the most important knowledge—knowledge of God—always brings with it humility rather than pride. To know God is to love him.

Of course, Paul adds, there is only one real God (v. 4), which, based on verse 1, we understand the Corinthians already knew from the Old Testament: "Hear O Israel, the LORD our God, the LORD is one" (Deut. 6:4) and from the powerful words of Isaiah, "'To whom will you compare me? Or who is my equal?' says the Holy One. Lift your eyes and look to the heavens: Who created all these? He who brings out the starry host one by one, and calls them each by name" (40:25–26).

Paul writes, "For even if there are so-called gods, whether in heaven or on earth (as indeed there are many "gods" and many "lords"), yet for us there is but one God, the Father, from whom all things came and for whom we live; and there is but one Lord, Jesus Christ, through whom all things came and through whom we live" (1 Cor. 8:5–6). In saying that there are many so-called gods, Paul is not renouncing monotheism. He is simply acknowledging the claims—false though they are—that many believe that there are other gods, particularly the pagan gods such as Hermes and Artemis and Apollo. Yet for us, Paul says, there is but one. Paul is not implying that other gods exist; rather, he is merely pointing out that the pagans all around them think that they do. Contrarily, the Corinthian Christians have been taught the truth—there is only one God—and it is from this truth that their problem springs. The believers in Corinth needed more than just the truth about knowledge; they also needed the truth about love.

The Truth about Love

Paul instructs the Corinthian believers that love for their brothers and sisters should guide their knowledge about food and their exercise of freedoms and rights: "Some people are still so accustomed to idols that when they eat such food they think of it as having been sacrificed to an idol, and since their conscience is weak, it is defiled. But food does not bring us near to God; we are no worse if we do not eat, and no better if we do" (vv. 7b–8).

An understanding of the food Paul mentions is key for our understanding of this passage. The food that was being served came from animal sacrifices to idols; some considered the food to be defiled as a result. Those who saw the food as defiled believed it was sinful to eat it because it had been sacrificed to idols, so for them it was sinful. The food becomes defiled not strictly because of the idol, but because of how the food was *viewed*. Writing later to the Roman Christians, Paul states, "The man who has doubts is condemned if he eats, because his eating is not from faith; and everything that does not come from faith is sin" (Rom. 14:23).

The consciences of some in Corinth were weak; due to lack of instruction their consciences were inaccurate guides about what constituted sin in this matter of food. Perhaps the young believers in Corinth were feeling the sharpness of their initial conviction about worshiping false gods. Even today there are members in our congregations who come from religions that use statues or practice other religious customs, and for them, such matters are live issues.

We sometimes forget how radically atheistic Christians seemed in the first century because they did not worship using images. The rules and scruples may have been unnecessary for the "weaker brother" Paul mentions here, but those rules and scruples were tied to very real intentions such as desire to honor the one true God. Their consciences were, as Paul says here, weak, but it is a dangerous thing to go against conscience. So the rightness of an action can, in part, depend on how we interpret it.

Of course, as Paul makes clear here, food itself is spiritually neutral. Paul's principles certainly do not apply to things that are not neutral—to things we are expressly commanded to do or not do. We cannot decide, for example, for conscience's sake, not to worship God or to commit adultery.

Understanding Weakness

In addition to educating the believers in Corinth about food, he teaches them about weakness, specifically, that by exercising their freedom to eat food that had been sacrificed to idols they might hurt the weak:

> Be careful, however, that the exercise of your freedom does not become a stumbling block to the weak. For if anyone with a weak conscience sees you who have this knowledge eating in an idol's temple, won't he be emboldened to eat what has been sacrificed to idols? So this weak brother, for whom Christ died, is destroyed by your knowledge. When you sin against your brothers in this way and wound their weak conscience, you sin against Christ. Therefore, if what I eat causes my brother to fall into sin, I will never eat meat again, so that I will not cause him to fall. (vv. 9–13)

Paul is not forbidding them from every exercise of freedom, but the effect their actions might have on others must be considered in all matters. There were great public feasts, such as those held before the Isthmian Games, in which participation was impossible without eating food that had been or was being offered to idols. The Isthmian Games were one of the Panhellenic games of ancient Greece, and they were held at the isthmus of Corinth every two years in honor of various gods such as Melicertes and Poseidon. Since these feasts were public, everyone could see what participants were eating and might attribute a participant's presence there as an assent to pagan worship. Paul's point is that, through one believer's example, a weak brother might be emboldened to do something that he understands as sinful. In such a situation, the knowledge that the participant has, which makes his participation acceptable, might hurt a weak brother. The exercise of one's freedom and rights might confuse the weaker brother, whose conscience, though in need of education, is as yet uneducated. Such confusion could well lead this weaker brother to sin against his own conscience, or into an indifference about actual sins, because of what he perceives as indifference in his brother. The weaker brother might even relapse into paganism. To show how seriously this consideration should be taken, Paul says that to sin against one's brothers in this way is to sin against Christ (cf. Acts 9:1–4).

We need to hear both sides of this. On the one hand, conscience should normally be obeyed as well as continually instructed by Scripture. On the other hand, we must consider the effects of our actions on other Christians, because God will. He takes our actions personally. Remember Jesus' teaching in Matthew 25:40: "Whatever you did for one of the least of these brothers of mine, you did for me." That is why Paul was glad to forego rights and freedoms; he sought to protect weaker brothers (cf. Rom. 14:19). Paul is such a good example in this! Giving up your rights for the good of others is Christlike.

If you are not a Christian, I wonder how all this sounds to you. Have you realized that you were not made to care *only* about yourself? For that matter, you were not made to care even *primarily* about yourself. In the same way that we are born utterly dependent on our parents for survival and dependent on our spouse for sexual union, we were designed to be spiritually dependent on someone else—on God himself. But, according to the Bible, we have each sinned and separated ourselves from God. We have rejected him by choosing to be our own lords, and this self-centeredness leaves us open to the certain judgment of God, who will one day judge us all. We are made in his image, and in judging us he will display his glory by vindicating his character.

If you are a Christian, let me urge you to take these principles to heart. Because we are prone to a weak conscience, we should be on a constant quest to educate ourselves and our conscience, which we do by reading our Bible and praying. We do so by becoming a member of a church where the Bible is rightly taught. We do so by making ourselves known—honestly known—to others in discipling relationships. We do so by investing in good books and reading them. We must see to it that our conscience is biblically educated and instructed. This practice concerns no one else so nearly as it does ourselves.

Pertaining to issues of behavior about which Christians disagree, we must ask whether we are more interested in using our liberty to prove that we are saved by grace or in thinking of how our freedoms and rights to drink something or to date someone will affect others around us. Think for a moment: in what way is *your* knowledge—or how you live because of your knowledge—in danger of harming other Christians? How does love guide your knowledge? Do you understand that sinning against your brother *is* sinning against Christ? The risen Christ said to Paul, back when he was known as Saul and was persecuting Christians in Damascus, "Why do you persecute me?" (Acts 9:4).

In our congregation, we have tried to recognize the corporate nature of our discipleship in our church covenant:

> We will work and pray for the unity of the Spirit in the bond of peace. We will walk together in brotherly love, as becomes the members of a Christian Church; exercise an affectionate care and watchfulness over each other and faithfully admonish and entreat one another as occasion may require. . . . We will rejoice at each other's happiness, and endeavor with tenderness and sympathy to bear each other's burdens and sorrows.

We want all growth in knowledge that we gain here to be captured in a growth of love. On a practical level, this means we are always thinking about how younger Christians would perceive our actions. It is amazing, isn't it, how the truths of sin, love, and church membership all hang together? The bottom line is this: we learn obedience by good teaching, and knowledge should be guided by love.

Obedience by Example

Paul continues the epistle by setting forth another way we learn obedience—through a good example (9:1–23). Paul desires to be an example, so in love he sets aside the freedoms that he knows he has for the sake of the gospel.

Not until a few years ago, when studying chapter 9, did I finally understand what 1 Corinthians as a whole is all about. It is in this chapter that we find Paul defending the way he has conducted his apostleship, and as I focused on his words, I began to see his discussion about his life as an apostle as an example of laying aside rights for the good of others. In discussing his apostleship, he is simply providing an application of the general principle of acting for the good of others.

Paul provided another application in the first four chapters of the epistle where he recounted his selfless desires for the edification of the whole at the cost of selfish ambitions, doing all he could to prevent the church from dividing over preferences for one teacher over another.

Throughout the letter, we see examples of Paul's acting for the good of others. We find it in his discussion about church discipline in chapter 5, again in his willingness to be wronged in chapter 6, and in his discussion about morality in chapters 6 and 7. His defense of the resurrection in chapter 15 protects the importance of obedience in the body. (Some people at the time assumed that at death one is forever done with the body, and they reasoned backward that sins committed in the body therefore have no ultimate significance. Paul's assertion of the resurrection of the body would have been a shock to any such satisfied sinners!) Paul's consideration of others before himself is what he exhorts the Corinthians to emulate in their services together. We see this in chapters 11 and 14. We see it again in chapters 12 and 14 in how they are to use their gifts, and yet again in chapter 16 in a concern for God's people everywhere. His commitment to the welfare of others finds its core in the love described and enjoined in chapter 13. In all of these ways, Paul serves as our example.

Here in chapter 9 we see Paul present himself to the Corinthians as a model of one whose knowledge is guided by love, and in doing so he makes four basic points. First, he is a model by virtue of his apostleship; second, because he is an apostle, he has a right to support; however, third, he has not exercised those rights among them because, fourth, he wants the gospel preached freely.

Paul Is a Model

First, then, Paul serves as a model in his role as an apostle. He writes, "Am I not free? Am I not an apostle? Have I not seen Jesus our Lord? Are you not the result of my work in the Lord? Even though I may not be an apostle to others, surely I am to you! For you are the seal of my apostleship in the Lord. This is my defense to those who sit in judgment on me" (vv. 1–3).

Here Paul is defending his credentials. As an apostle he is certainly free. He is a witness to the living Christ because on the Damascus Road Christ did appear to Paul. Surely, of all people, the Corinthians ought to recognize him as an apostle since he is the one who first brought the gospel to them. That was how he defended himself to his detractors. But his point here is not so much defending himself as it is simply to demonstrate that he has a right to support.

Paul Has a Right to Support

As an apostle, Paul has a right to support (vv. 4–11), the same right as that of the other apostles. "Don't we have the right to food and drink?" he asks. "Don't we have the right to take a believing wife along with us, as do the other apostles and the Lord's brothers and Cephas? Or is it only I and Barnabas who must work for a living?" (vv. 4–6). He certainly has the right to food and drink, and in verse 5 he points out that all the apostles have the right to a wife and the right to travel with her. So, Paul reasons, he has the right to be supported by preaching the gospel. He gives more reasons for this right:

> Who serves as a soldier at his own expense? Who plants a vineyard and does not eat of its grapes? Who tends a flock and does not drink of the milk? Do I say this merely from a human point of view? Doesn't the Law say the same thing? For it is written in the Law of Moses: "Do not muzzle an ox while it is treading out the grain." (vv. 7–9)

The support Paul is describing is common custom, as can be seen from his three examples of workers being supported by the fruits of their work, and it has biblical backing. He shows in verse 8 that Old Testament law teaches it. In verse 9 Paul quotes Deuteronomy 25:4, his point being that people should be paid for their work. Experience confirms that this is and should continue to be the case for workers. Therefore, Paul is entitled to material pay for his spiritual work among them.

Paul Forfeits His Rights

No sooner has Paul established his right to support then he turns around and forfeits it:

> If others have this right of support from you, shouldn't we have it all the more? But we did not use this right. On the contrary, we put up with anything rather than hinder the gospel of Christ. Don't you know that those who work in the temple get their food from the temple, and those who serve at the altar share in what is offered on the altar? In the same way, the Lord has commanded that those who preach the gospel should receive their living from the gospel. But I have not used any of these rights. And I am not writing this in the hope that you will do such things for me. I would rather die than have anyone deprive me of this boast. (vv. 12–15)

Paul references the support given to priests, and those who work in the temple get their food from the temple. Yes, he has a right to support, but he has not availed himself of it. For the sake of the gospel Paul didn't use this right. But why didn't he use his right in Corinth, when we know that he did elsewhere? Perhaps Paul wanted to distance himself from the orators who came and made a living speaking to the rich *for a price.*

Paul's words provide good arguments for why churches should provide a comfortable maintenance for pastors and their families, one that will allow them to do what God has called them to do in the church and beyond it. Paul taught the same principle to the Galatians: "Anyone who receives instruction in the word must share all good things with his instructor" (Gal. 6:6; cf. 1 Tim. 5:17–18). Most importantly, Jesus is the one who established the principle when he said, "The worker deserves his wages" (Luke 10:7; cf. Matt. 10:10). Money that the church spends on staff is one of its best investments.

Paul reiterates in verse 15 that he has not nor does he want to use this right. He is careful to guard against a misunderstanding as to why he has raised the issue of support. He is not attempting to drop a subtle hint. Again, what he is doing is expressing eagerness to give up his support in exchange for the freedom to preach the gospel unhindered. He presents his own life as an example of the knowledge that is to be sought in the service of love, which is the exhortation he began back in chapter 8.

Paul preaches not to make money but to obey God. Paul feels compelled. Surely in every God-called minister there is a willingness that presses into a compulsion to preach. Samuel Jones described it as "the inward call, which is a zeal for the glory of God in the salvation of the souls of men, and a strong desire to be made useful in that way, with a persuasion of God's designation of the person for the office. This is the voice of God in his conscience."[1] And this is how Paul understands his preaching; he is discharging the trust committed to him (cf. 4:1). The reward Paul receives is simply the ability to offer the gospel free of charge. He finds great satisfaction in forgoing his rights for this purpose.

Furthermore, preaching freely testified to the truth and the importance and even the very nature of his message. "Though I am free and belong to no man, I make myself a slave to everyone, to win as many as possible" (v. 19). Paul is free, but he makes himself a slave to all to win all. He is bound to do whatever will further the gospel and build the church (cf. Jesus in Phil. 2:7–8). Paul becomes a Jew to the Jews in order to win them (v. 20). By "becoming a Jew," Paul is not implying that he has placed himself under the covenant of works; rather, in order to win Jews, he adopts Jewish customs. Paul also says that he becomes a Gentile to the Gentiles (v. 21). He is under Christ's law, that is, the law of God, which is not exactly the same as the Old Testament law. So Paul does whatever he can, regardless of his rights, to win whomever he can. Paul's motivation is to win people to Christ.

Paul gives himself and his rights to win others, to be a blessing and an encouragement to people.

Who, in your life, has been an example of selflessness? I am not implying that we are wrong to avail ourselves of civic tools such as a bill of rights or other basic human rights. Paul isn't writing here as a citizen of the earthly kingdom so much as a citizen of the heavenly kingdom. In the heavenly community, sacrificing our rights is a Christlike thing to do because it is what Christ did. Jesus was God incarnate. He committed no sins, and yet he died the death of sinners, paying the penalty for our sin before God. God raised him from this death, and so Jesus Christ became the risen Lord of his people.

So, brothers and sisters, do we see such examples of giving up rights for others in our own congregations? Have we experienced the blessing of giving up our rights for others? There are so many rights to reconsider in light of the urgency of the gospel! What rights are you not willing to give up for the good of others? Your Sunday evenings? Time with your friends? A particular kind of music? Your home country? Your desire to do what you want whenever you want to do it? An expectation that God will make everything work out okay for your family? Your health? Your sleep? Perhaps the right you are called to reexamine has to do with where you live. Perhaps you are reconsidering your rights to your career, your money, certain circumstances in your marriage, your requirement of a spouse, your use of alcohol, or spending so much time traveling on weekends that your church cannot be built on you as it should be. Opportunities to minister fall to others, to those who will give themselves away for the sake of others and for the glory of God.

As a church, we want to pray to have a culture of humble, self-giving, encouraging love. We want to have leaders who are pronounced in laying aside selfish considerations for the good of others. We want to follow Paul's example in inconveniencing ourselves to make the gospel known to others. We want to go to places we otherwise wouldn't go. We want to learn things we wouldn't learn, and meet people we otherwise might not meet. This is why we do small-group Bible studies with people, and get to know folks at restaurants, and strike up conversations on airplanes, and have talks at Starbucks.

Sunday mornings are not particularly the time to be seeker sensitive. Sundays are the time to gather as a family, a body, though visitors are certainly welcome. But our lives should be seeker sensitive, not wanting to give unnecessary offense, desiring to be winsome in our lives and witness and testimony. Like Paul, we want to participate in the blessings of salvation and in the blessing of being instruments through which other sinners are saved and God is thereby glorified. Brothers and sisters, arrange your life to share the gospel, and enjoy the freedom that comes to you as you watch others being freed from the penalty of their sins and reconciled to God.

We learn obedience by a good example—Paul—who in love set aside his freedoms and rights for the sake of the gospel.

Obedience by Bad Example (9:24–10:13)

The third way we learn obedience is by observing the awful results of disobedience. Paul provides the Corinthians with an example of falling to the temptation to disobey. But before launching into the bad example, Paul exhorts the Corinthians to follow his good example of working hard for a good reason:

> Do you not know that in a race all the runners run, but only one gets the prize? Run in such a way as to get the prize. Everyone who competes in the games goes into strict training. They do it to get a crown that will not last; but we do it to get a crown that will last forever. Therefore I do not run like a man running aimlessly; I do not fight like a man beating the air. No, I beat my body and make it my slave so that after I have preached to others, I myself will not be disqualified for the prize. (vv. 24–27)

Paul encourages the Corinthians to run to get the prize, perhaps again drawing the image from the great Isthmian Games held near Corinth. He reminds them that if athletes work hard to gain a passing crown (in the Isthmian Games the victory wreath was made of small pine branches), we should work even harder to gain an everlasting crown. Paul does not run or fight to no purpose; he doesn't want to waste his efforts. He seems to be referring to the danger in Corinth—a danger today as well—of believers giving in to sexual temptation and disobeying God. And with that, he turns to his bad example, the account of the exodus in the Old Testament:

For I do not want you to be ignorant of the fact, brothers, that our forefathers were all under the cloud and that they all passed through the sea. They were all baptized into Moses in the cloud and in the sea. They all ate the same spiritual food and drank the same spiritual drink; for they drank from the spiritual rock that accompanied them, and that rock was Christ. (1 Cor. 10:1–4)

Paul reminds the Corinthians that their forefathers had known great blessings from God and were well acquainted with God's power. The Israelites had been baptized into Moses by means of going through the cloud and the sea. These passages were types of baptism (see Ex. 13:21–22; 14:19, 21–31). The Israelites had been immersed into the people of God under Moses' leadership and therefore immersed under the law God gave through him. Moses had been the agent of God's deliverance of his people.

The Israelites had spiritual food and spiritual drink, and Christ was the spiritual rock from which they drank—facts Paul draws from the books of Exodus and Numbers (Ex. 16:15, 35; 17:1–7; Num. 20:1–13). The fact that the rock from which the Israelites drank symbolized Christ is perhaps why God was so concerned that Moses strike that rock with his staff only once and no more; Christ was struck only once, and then never again.

Paul makes clear that the Israelites had been the recipients of great blessing, and he uses this as the introduction to a warning. Despite all their blessings, the Israelites, the forefathers of the Corinthians, disobeyed:

Nevertheless, God was not pleased with most of them; their bodies were scattered over the desert. Now these things occurred as examples to keep us from setting our hearts on evil things as they did. Do not be idolaters, as some of them were; as it is written: "The people sat down to eat and drink and got up to indulge in pagan revelry." We should not commit sexual immorality, as some of them did—and in one day twenty-three thousand of them died. We should not test the Lord, as some of them did—and were killed by snakes. And do not grumble, as some of them did—and were killed by the destroying angel. These things happened to them as examples and were written down as warnings for us, on whom the fulfillment of the ages has come. (vv. 5–11)

Even after all that blessing, God killed some of them. They are examples to us not to set our heart on evil things (See Num. 11:4–34.) The Old Testament is rich in redemptive-historical meaning, yet it also provides models of encouragement and warning. The Old Testament is not merely exemplary, but it is not less than exemplary. Paul issues four specific warnings from the Israelite example:

(1) Avoid idolatry (see Ex. 32:1–6). Paul's warning certainly contained echoes of the Corinthian feasts.

(2) Avoid sexual immorality. Licentiousness was common at Corinthian feasts (See Num. 25:1–9); is it common in our congregations as well?

(3) Do not test the Lord (See Ex. 17:2; Num. 21:4–9; Ps. 78:18.) Perhaps because nothing terrible had happened, some were saying that it was fine to eat at the pagan temples. But living to sin the same way a second day is no evidence that God is turning a blind eye. Do not relax into patterns of sin. Doubting God's goodness or ability is dangerous. Don Carson has described testing the Lord as "chronic and repeated unbelief 'with attitudes.'"[2] "Sinning with a high hand," is how the Puritans described it. Brother and sisters, do we sin with attitude in our congregations?

(4) Do not grumble (see Num. 14:2; 16:41–50). Perhaps some of the Corinthian Christians were grumbling about the difficulty of living the Christian life in pagan Corinth. The sort of grumbling referred to here is no mere expression of sadness or even depression. Paul is not describing a fundamentally emotional state or a one-time complaint. The grumbling here is the sort that is openly distrustful and disobedient. How do we deal with the temptation to distrustful disobedience? We do so by looking at the big picture, just as Paul is doing here in the epistle.

The Israelites are examples—negative examples—of the warning of God's judgment on self-centered sin. The Old Testament was written not just for its first and immediate audience, but also for us, for Christians today, and this portion of the Old Testament story acts as a warning to us.

Back in chapter 7 Paul had instructed the Corinthians that Christians are to warn and admonish one another. One way we do this is by remembering the Old Testament Israelites. We ought to do so when considering our own hearts and when we consider our weaker brothers who are just being delivered from sin. We must be careful that we do not harden our hearts to them, and that we take into consideration how our actions will affect them.

We are to beware of temptation, and we are to guard ourselves against overconfidence. Paul continues, "If you think you are standing firm, be careful that you don't fall! No temptation has seized you except what is common to man. And God is faithful; he will not let you be tempted beyond what you can bear. But when you are tempted, he will also provide a way out so that you can stand up under it" (vv. 12–13).

Paul is careful to warn those believers in Corinth who were eating at the feasts in the temples. Receiving baptism and taking communion provide no final security against God's judgment for a life lived in licentiousness. The fruit of the Spirit will appear in the life of a Christian. Be careful.

At the same time we are to guard against overconfidence, we can be rightly confident that God will enable us to resist any temptation. You face the temptations common to all people. And you can outlast all of them, with God's help. Oh, my brothers and sisters in Christ, what good has come out of the sin in your life? Do not follow the bad examples you have seen around you. Learn from them instead. You may not—you will not—be able to avoid temptation, but you will never find a temptation that, by God's grace, is unendurable.

We are reminded through this story that the starting line and the finishing line are not the same thing. Some who have witnessed God's great acts have, instead of responding in humility, persisted in their sin and unbelief. We must not be one of those. If you are one of them—one who has confessed Christ, been baptized, and resolved not to be left in the desert—trust God, keep trusting God, and follow his direction. Plan well to be in church here or church in heaven, but plan never to be far away from a meeting of God's saints. Learn from the sad examples of those who have fallen from the faith. Take note of their examples and avoid their fate by avoiding their sins.

Our churches cannot coast in spiritual things. Regardless of what amazing things we have seen God do in our congregation, we must continue to rely upon him daily for fresh deliverances. Let us pray that we see a growing, thriving church culture in which we encourage one another in self-control and exult in God's good and kind providences to us. Let us learn obedience, even by bad example.

Conclusion

After reviewing Paul's warning, do you feel freshly resolved to obey God, even if it means laying down some of your own preferences, your own rights, as Paul did—even if doing so means laying down your life?

Hugh and Nicholas had to rely upon God for fresh deliverances in one particular trial they faced together. They learned firsthand Paul's words, "No temptation has seized you except what is common to man. And God is faithful; he will not let you be tempted beyond what you can bear. But when you are tempted, he will also provide a way out so that you can stand up under it."

In 1553 Edward VI died, and his Roman Catholic half-sister Mary Tudor became queen. She immediately arrested Hugh and put him in the Tower of London. Nicholas was removed from being a bishop and excommunicated. Eventually they were both brought to Oxford for trial where they were found guilty of believing in salvation through Christ alone by faith alone. Because they would not renounce this knowledge, they were sentenced to die.

After some weeks of separate imprisonment, the two met on the day that they were to be executed. They were led to a certain place in Oxford where a crowd had gathered. Nicholas Ridley, the younger of the two, distributed some mementos. Hugh Latimer, seventy years old, was stripped down to his shroud. Men wept at the scene. A blacksmith took the two preachers and fastened them to a large stake with a chain. They piled logs around them. Nicholas Ridley's brother-in-law was allowed to give each one bags of gunpowder with the intention that the ensuing explosion would shorten their sufferings. Someone brought fire and began the flame at Ridley's feet. Latimer then said to him, "Be of good comfort, Master Ridley, and play the man. We shall this day light such a candle, by God's grace, in England, as I trust shall never be put out."

The flames grew quickly. Hugh Latimer prayed, "Father of heaven, receive my soul," and he swiftly died, perhaps from suffocation. Nicholas Ridley's death took longer. The fire quickly hurt him but slowly killed him.

Such dramatic deaths for the gospel of justification may seem unrelated to the smaller matters of giving up your rights for the good of someone else. But I think they are related. The heart that is prepared to value God, the gospel, and others ahead of self in the little ways is the heart ready to serve God in the bigger ways that days ahead might call for.

By God's grace, Latimer and Ridley's love for the truth exceeded their love for their lives. It was more than 450 years ago that Hugh Latimer and Nicholas Ridley were burned to death in Oxford for the gospel, but we can keep their example alive today as we hear and enjoy the gospel of Jesus Christ. Thank God for the light they lit, that we still, in part, share in today.

Realize that it is the small acts of self-giving love and obedience that prepare you for the grander ones. Preferences and even rights surrendered in love make way for a life surrendered in love.

7

LEGALISM

1 CORINTHIANS 10:14–11:1

Every person operating a bus line in the city shall provide equal but separate accommodations for white people and Negroes on his buses, by requiring the employees in charge thereof to assign passengers seats on the vehicles under their charge in such manner as to separate the white people from the Negroes, where there are both white and Negroes on the same car; provided, however, that Negro nurses having in charge white children or sick or infirm white persons may be assigned seats among white people."

That was chapter 6, section 10 of the Montgomery, Alabama, city code. The next section, section 11, gave the bus drivers the power to enforce section 10. Such laws were only a few decades old, and this specific city ordinance had been on the books for only about three years. Privately held transportation services did not generate enough profit to run the risk of alienating a large segment of their customers, so the private companies did not mandate segregated seating. Everybody's money was green. But when publicly owned bus lines put the for-profit lines out of business, then segregated seating laws and ordinances came on the books as a result of whiter-than-thou politicking.

About 6:00 PM on Thursday, December 1, 1955, James Blake complained that Rosa Parks was sitting in the white section of the bus and was refusing to move. Four days later, she was tried on charges of disorderly conduct in violation of the local ordinance. Her trial lasted thirty minutes. Parks was found guilty and fined ten dollars, plus four dollars in court costs. Afterward a bus boycott was arranged, and for over a year the black citizens of Montgomery, Alabama, refused to ride the buses, often at great personal cost of time, difficulty, and energy, not to mention the hostility generated toward them.

On June 19, 1956, the U.S. District Court three-judge panel ruled that sections 10 and 11 of chapter 6 of the code of the city of Montgomery, 1952, "deny and deprive plaintiffs and other Negro citizens similarly situated of the equal protection of the laws and due process of law secured by the Fourteenth Amendment," (Browder v. Gayle, 1956). On November 13, 1956, the United States Supreme Court outlawed racial segregation on buses, deeming it unconstitutional. The court order arrived in Montgomery, Alabama, on December 20, 1956. The bus boycott ended on December 21, 1956. You know the rest of the story.

This matrix of concerns—law, love, sacrifice, freedom—has always been of special concern for Christians. God has revealed himself in law. Christians are called to respect the law of the land. Yet love sometimes mandates a higher calling. Obedience to such a higher calling will often involve sacrifice, a giving up of our freedoms, in order to serve others. All of this is involved in the portion of 1 Corinthians that we will examine in this chapter.

Paul had planted the church at Corinth some months earlier, maybe even a year or two earlier, and he was writing this letter to encourage them about God's good work among them and to warn them not to trade the wisdom of the gospel for the passing wisdom of this world. The Corinthian congregation was in danger of accepting worldly teachers and worldly standards. Paul warned them that they had a responsibility to judge their teachers by their life and doctrine and to judge each other, as well as to give of themselves in caring for one another and to be willing to lay aside their rights to that end. Paul brings this last point, the laying aside of rights, to a conclusion in 1 Corinthians 10:14–11:1.

Here we find that the Christian life is not a life of legalism. Neither is it a life of licentious self-indulgence. It is a Christlike life. A Christlike life is marked supremely by self-sacrificial love lived out for the good of others. In this section, Paul gives the Corinthian Christians five instructions: (1) flee false gods; (2) seek the good of others; (3) recognize your freedom;

(4) forgo your freedoms for the good of others; and (5) live for the true God's glory.

I pray that as we study these passages together, we will come to understand more of God's love for us in Christ and that his love will more fully grip our hearts and intelligently shape our love.

Flee False Gods (10:14–22)

"Therefore, my dear friends, flee from idolatry," Paul writes (v. 14). Paul gives emphatic instruction to the Corinthians: flee the false gods! He says it clearly, even urgently, in much the same tone as his earlier exhortation to flee from sexual immorality (6:18). Paul was warning the Corinthians who were so certain of their spiritual strength and maturity not to eat in the pagan temples or at the public feasts. Paul's exhortation would have been a hard teaching for the Corinthians to bear because so much of the social and political life had to do with great public feasts. Such feasts were held at pagan temples, and much of the available food in Corinth came from the animals that had been publicly offered to the gods. Paul was cutting close to the bone here with his instructions. Maybe that's why he begins with an intense "dear friends."

He knows that his words will be hard for the Corinthians to hear and to adopt, which is why he calls them to think carefully about the issue: "I speak to sensible people; judge for yourselves what I say" (v. 15). He calls them to judge the matter carefully. This is the sort of judging with which they need to be engaged. Such judging aids in understanding the truth of a situation. Then, in order to persuade them to take the issue more seriously than some of them had been taking it, he gives them two examples—the Lord's Supper and the Old Testament Jewish sacrifices.

The Lord's Supper

"Is not the cup of thanksgiving for which we give thanks a participation in the blood of Christ? And is not the bread that we break a participation in the body of Christ?" (v. 16). Communion is participation in the body and blood of Christ. This verse has been interpreted in a variety of ways. Roman Catholics use it to show transubstantiation, the belief that the bread and wine become the body and blood of Christ while keeping only the appearance of bread and wine. Our Lutheran friends use it to show consubstantiation, the actual substantial presence and combination of the body and blood of Christ with the bread and wine. But the abstracted or changed substances of the bread and wine do not seem to be the point Paul is making. The point here seems to be the *effect* of sharing in them. We participate in the blood and body of Christ.

To receive the cup and bread rightly—that is, with true faith—is to receive Christ. We share in the benefits of his saving work on Calvary. At the cross, God's love took a particular form. At the cross God's wrath against sin and God's love for sinners was worked out. It was on the cross that God's love dealt with his own holiness and righteousness. Christ, in great suffering, took our sin upon himself and carried it away. The perfect God took on flesh, lived a perfect life, and died on the cross as a substitute, taking on the punishment for all the sinners who would ever repent of their sins and trust in God. And if we repent and believe, then Christ is our savior. Taking Communion—the Eucharist, the Lord's Supper—doesn't save you. Trusting in Christ and his death proclaimed in the supper *does*. In order to be saved, we do not need Christ's physical body ingested in us; we need Christ's righteousness accounted to us.

The Lord's Supper demonstrates that Christ's blood spilled and body broken on the cross are at the center of our fellowship. We are not united with one another unless we are first incorporated into Christ. As Paul goes on to say, "Because there is one loaf, we, who are many, are one body, for we all partake of the one loaf" (v. 17). Participating in one loaf makes us one people. We have the same Lord. Of course, the point here is not one literal loaf; the size of some of the churches we read about in the New Testament would have made that difficult. Rather, the point is the one kind of bread served at one simultaneous sitting. We have one meal, the symbol of one table, going out to multiple people, but it is singularly *the Lord's* table.

This is one reason why separate observances of Communion among subsets of a particular congregation are a distortion of its intention. The unity of the body, which Communion is meant to display, is obscured when just the youth group, or a couple at a wedding, or someone in the hospital, or some folks on a retreat or in a small group take Communion. We see here the serious sin that disunity is. We see also the importance of acting together and how sins affecting our unity must not be brought to the Lord's Table. Such sins particularly strike at what the Table symbolizes.

The Jewish Sacrifices

The second example Paul uses to show the Corinthians the link between eating meat sacrificed to idols with participating in pagan worship came from the Jewish sacrifices. The Jews participated in the sacrifices they offered by eating them (See Lev. 3:3; 7:15; 8:31; Deut. 12:18; 1 Sam. 9:10–24). The priest and the person offering the sacrifice would share in eating the offered meat. Paul goes on to say in verse 19 that idols are nothing, a point he made earlier in the letter (8:4), but the real point he is making here comes in verse 20: "The sacrifices of pagans are offered to demons, not to God, and I do not want you to be participants with demons." When Paul says that the sacrifices of pagans are offered to demons, he is simply treating idols as the prophets of the Old Testament did. (See Deut. 32:17; Ps. 106:37; cf. Gal. 4:8). Paul reasons that the Corinthians could not participate in the worship of both the Lord and demons (v. 21). Doing so is an impossibility. So, he continues, in verse 22, "Are we trying to arouse the Lord's jealousy? Are we stronger than he?" (v. 22).

The question in Greek presumes a negative answer, so be careful. Our actions will bring God's judgment on us, just as Israel's actions brought judgment on Israel. Be especially careful, those of you who recognize your liberty and strength; judge carefully here. We cannot survive a confrontation with God when he is against us (cf. Deut. 32:21; Isa. 42:8; James 4:4–5). We can imagine sneaking across the path of a sleeping lion if we *had* to, but why would we toy with the possibility of arousing the consuming wrath of God?

Brothers and sisters, if you have a religious background that includes worship by means of idols and images, Paul's teaching is directly applicable to you. Don't let your Christian understanding—which has liberated you from enslavement to images you now recognize as nothing more than wood, stone, or metal—be used as an excuse to ignore the spiritual reality behind them. If you do not come from such a background, what false gods are you tempted by? What do you talk about? What interests you? What excites you? Whatever you answer is what you worship. Flee idolatry, Paul says.

Seek the Good of Others

Paul's second instruction in this section is that believers must seek the good of others. 'Everything is permissible'—but not everything is beneficial. 'Everything is permissible'—but not everything is constructive. Nobody should seek his own good, but the good of others" (vv. 23–24). Here again Paul takes up the chant being used by some of the Corinthians and responds to it.

In this second of four instructions found in our passage, Paul moves from the good of those he is addressing to the consideration of the good they do to others. While eating idol-offered meat may be permissible, as the Corinthians kept asserting, it was not necessarily beneficial. In fact, it might even be destructive. Earlier Paul pointed out that there are times when a believer might be harmed through the exercise of liberty (6:12–13). Here in chapter 10 he calls the Corinthians to reflect on how their use of liberty might hurt others. In chapter 8 Paul wrote, "If anyone with a weak conscience sees you who have this knowledge eating in an idol's temple, won't he be emboldened to eat what has been sacrificed to idols?" We must avoid actions that are so destructive to others. This is why Paul has just finished cautioning them, "If you think you are standing firm, be careful that you don't fall" (10:12). Here again we have an example not of liberty being destroyed—Paul has just defended it, and is about to do so again—but an example of liberty being guided by love.

"Nobody should seek his own good, but the good of others" he continues (v. 24). Seek the good of others; govern your behavior by what is good for them. He will make this argument again when he writes to the Romans (see Rom. 14:13, 15, 19; 15:1–2). Jesus had reminded his disciples of the importance of this teaching from Leviticus 19:18: "Love your neighbor as yourself." In fact, Jesus said that this was one of the most important of God's commands (see Matt. 22:39). The good of others is to determine our actions. We are to love others as Christ has loved us.

As I mentioned earlier, this was a hard teaching for the Corinthians. Eating meat sacrificed to idols at civic feasts, in lavish temples, and at public events was to great social advantage in Corinth. Yet all of this, Paul says, should be forfeited. The Christian's main concern is the benefit of others rather than the advance of self.

I wonder how that sounds to you? All around us today we hear religious versions of "look out for number one." Who is number one in your life? Do you put others' needs before your own, perhaps your parents' or your children's? Perhaps a spouse's or a friend's? All of those natural relationships that require personal sacrifice are really reminders, pointers, to God and his love for us in Christ. Christ lived—and died—for the good of others.

Let us consider carefully Paul's instruction. When we have settled in our minds that something is not wrong in and of itself, that is, that we have liberty to do it, we must still answer the question about whether the action is right or wrong in a particular circumstance or at a particular time. So how are you seeking the good of others? How have you altered your plans in the last week—large or small—in order to do what was best for others?

This is an important matter to consider in our churches, in everything from how we plan our public worship services to how we practice tithing. The local church is a great context in which to serve others. We must work to help each other defeat our consumerist impulse to be served at church and instead labor to help one another and to give ourselves in love. We want to be a church marked by seeking the good of others.

Realize Your Freedom (10:25–27)

Paul acknowledges an important, even foundational, truth about Christian freedom when he writes, "Eat anything sold in the meat market without raising questions of conscience, for, 'The earth is the Lord's, and everything in it.' If some unbeliever invites you to a meal and you want to go, eat whatever is put before you without raising questions of conscience" (v. 25). This is the third of four instructions we find in this portion of the epistle.

Here Paul is making room for one of the Corinthians' major assertions. Christians, Paul says, have the freedom to eat anything. The Corinthians were free to eat anything sold in the market. The market in ancient Corinth, as in other cities, was where one went to get meat. The meat found there had, as I noted earlier, most likely come from sacrifices offered in one of the city temples. Some of the offered meat was eaten by the one giving the offering, still more of it by the priest; but much of it, perhaps most of it, was butchered and sold, with the proceeds supporting the temple and its priests.

Those shopping at the market rarely knew the source of the food they were buying. But they did not really need to know because, says Paul, citing Psalm 24:1, "The earth is the Lord's and everything in it" (v. 26). This was a well-known verse among first-century Jews. It was recited by many of the pious before eating. It served as a pre-meal prayer, acknowledging the Lord for his provision (cf. Pss. 50:12; 89:11). God alone is the source of the meat. Jesus, too, taught, "Don't you see that nothing that enters a man from the outside can make him 'unclean'? For it doesn't go into his heart but into his stomach, and then out of his body" (Mark 7:18–19). And in a vision God said to Peter, "Don't call anything impure that God has made" (Acts 10:15).

So Paul could agree with the Corinthians' assertion, telling them to eat anything put before them at the table of an unbeliever.

Today, as always, our food comes to us by the hand of God. Apart from him, we would have nothing, and in acknowledging this truth, eating can become an act of worship. On the other hand, if you're not a Christian, even eating your lunch will be accepting provisions from your Enemy.

Food laws, which are a part of so many religions, are not part of Christianity, a fact that well represents the gospel of Jesus Christ as a gospel for everyone, in every place, across all cultures. In our churches we want to teach the liberty that a Christian has in such matters, because teaching about liberty clearly protects the gospel. There is no place for the little legalisms we allow to creep in and attach themselves to the free gospel, and they should have no place in our life together. We don't want to forbid what Scripture allows. Instead, we want to encourage the responsible, joyful use of God's creation as a way of worshiping him. The beauty of God's creation is meant to be a reflection of God's character. Realize that we are free!

Forgo Your Freedoms

The fourth instruction we find in this portion of Paul's epistle is to forgo our freedoms for the good of others. "If anyone says to you, 'This has been offered in sacrifice,' then do not eat it, both for the sake of the man who told you and for conscience' sake—the other man's conscience, I mean, not yours. For why should my freedom be judged by another's conscience? If I take part in the meal with thankfulness, why am I denounced because of something I thank God for?" (vv. 28–30).

We come to the section that in one sense can be most difficult to understand, particularly verse 29. Verse 28 is straightforward: if your host tells you that the meat you are about to eat has been sacrificed to an idol, do not eat the meat, Paul says. In this way you serve as a witness to those in the home at which you are eating. To eat the meat would appear to be countenancing and approving of idolatry, either before non-Christians or before young Christians who might not yet have fully understood the implications of Psalm 24:1.

Paul has just finished telling the Corinthians that they are free to eat such meat in their own homes and even at someone else's home, but now he makes an exception. If your host tells you that the meat has been sacrificed to idols then you shouldn't eat it. Okay, no problem. Then Paul says you should abstain for the sake of the conscience of the one who told you the origin of the meal. That still makes sense. But then comes the difficult part, where Paul asks, "Why should my freedom be judged by another's conscience? That sounds like an *objection* to his freedom that is being imposed by the conscience of the other. How can Paul write these words just after telling the Corinthian Christians to govern the use of their freedoms according to the conscience of another?

Two basic explanations are given. The first is that verse 28 and the first half of verse 29 are a parenthesis expressing an exception to the exercise of Christian freedom. The statement is viewed as a disjunction, which it is meant to be. The other explanation is that Paul is thinking of the idea of being judged in the sense of being *controlled* by the conscience of another. He is not controlled by someone else; instead, he chooses to lay down his rights when those freedoms and rights are opposed to the good of someone else.

Either way, Paul clearly makes an appeal to the Corinthians to forgo their freedom in the case of the man who informs them that this meat has been sacrificed to idols. Paul wants the Corinthian Christians to determine their actions by what would be of most help to their non-Christian friends. Eating the meat might confuse unbelievers about the gospel. They might think that Christianity includes idol worship, allowing Christians to participate in it. This misconception might make Jesus appear to be just another addition to the pantheon of pagan gods. Let your actions be determined by what will help your non-Christian host.

The correct response to such a situation is not the establishing of another law, nor is it the restriction of this freedom in an absolute sense. Because, as Paul has just argued, the meat itself is pure. It is from God and can therefore be eaten in thanks to God. However, the decision must be based on the needs of the dinner host and on the truth of the gospel; refraining is best if eating the meat might blur this truth.

A legalistic response to such situations is to classify something as wrong in all situations; however, the answer Paul gives here is not legalistic. It is an answer springing from the loving use or nonuse of a Christian's freedoms, always having in mind the good of the other. Paul wants to make sure that no one mistakes what he is doing by his eating (v. 30)—he's worshiping God and giving thanks to him. He is not worshiping a demon!

We are called to modify how we behave in order to avoid confusing unbelievers about what it means to be a Christian. We desire others to understand the gospel by our words and lives, so we will work to try to be accurate messengers of the great news about Jesus Christ. We want our unbelieving friends to have a restored relationship with God, and we want them to know that this is our intention—something much more important than our comfort and convenience.

How can you use your freedoms for the gospel? Every situation you face comes with an opportunity. Are you willing to be flexible and to inconvenience yourself in order to help others come to grasp the gospel? What freedoms are you unwilling to forgo in order to share the gospel with others? Do you have to be able to drink that, or wear this, or shop here, or own that? What if those things might confuse the Muslim or the Mormon or the backslidden Baptist with whom you are sharing the gospel? Is your priority the exercising of your freedoms or reaching the lost?

In our congregations, too, we want to discourage actions that might lead to division among us. We want to encourage edification and the pattern of acting for the good of others. For some, this will affect the way that we think about drinking; for others, it may alter our conversations about politics that assume that everyone shares our positions. We want to be congregations that forgo our freedoms for the good of others.

Live for God's Glory

Paul's fifth instruction in this section is that we are to live for the glory of God. "So whether you eat or drink or whatever you do, do it all for the glory of God" (v. 31). Brothers and sisters, flee idolatry, and instead live for the true God's glory. Love others for God's glory. Benefit others by following the examples of Paul and Christ who set aside their freedoms. This is how you can worship the true God.

In all we eat and drink and do, we are to do everything for the glory of God. Even our eating is set apart to the glory of God. Our desire to glorify God by blessing others outweighs our desire to eat the meat Paul describes. God is glorified as his worth is evidenced and shown. As Paul writes later to the Colossians, "Whatever you do, whether in word or deed, do it all in the name of the Lord Jesus, giving thanks to God the Father through him" (Col. 3:17; cf. 1 Pet. 4:11).

How do we glorify God? We discover and expose his character, his actions, his holiness, and his love. We broadcast his love in Christ. We tell the truth about him, and the truth about God is glorious! He doesn't need any makeup. There is no need to distort the truth about God or to lie about him. Let's give ourselves to this great work. Spurgeon said, "While we can serve God, let us recollect that the time may come when we shall rather have to bear than to do; when we can only glorify him by suffering, and not by earnest activity."[1]

The founder of George Washington University, Luther Rice, "was an exponent of the current orthodox theology of his day. The attributes (especially the sovereignty) of God, human depravity, and the atonement, with allied themes, were the chief subjects of his addresses; but above all else, the glory of God."[2] One contemporary said about him:

> Well do I remember the impressions made upon my mind the first time I ever heard him preach. I could not refrain from remarking subsequently, to several brethren, that he seemed to keep the glory of God more distinctly in view, in his preaching, than any individual I had ever before heard. This was his great, his peculiar characteristic—a thirsting for the advancement of the glory of God.[3]

Paul instructed the Corinthians, "Do not cause anyone to stumble, whether Jews, Greeks or the church of God" (v. 32). In other words, do not act in such a way as to cause people to misunderstand the gospel—not Jews or Greeks or other Christians. This is the same principle that inspired Paul's actions of which he spoke earlier:

> To the Jews I became like a Jew, to win the Jews. To those under the law I became like one under the law (though I myself am not under the law), so as to win those under the law. To those not having the law I became like one not having the law (though I am not free from God's law but am under Christ's law), so as to win those not having the law. (9:20–21)

He sums up his views and his approach to life, writing, "For I am not seeking my own good but the good of many, so that they may be saved" (v. 33). Paul presents himself as a model for us in this.

However, this doesn't mean that we live to please others for the sake of our own self-advancement. Such man-pleasing is routinely condemned in Scripture, and it tends to hurt rather than benefit both ourselves and the one we would please. It hurts us because the pleasure of the one whose favor we are seeking becomes our goal rather than that person's good. Our ultimate goal should always be the pleasure of God. It also hurts the very ones we want to please because it gives them a sort of godlike influence over our actions, something they were never meant to have and which they cannot use well, and which only deludes them as to their own status and place in the scheme of things. God alone is to have that place, just as the apostles said to the Sanhedrin when they were exhorted to preach no more in the name of Jesus: "We must obey God rather than men" (Acts 5:29; cf. 4:19).

Let's not delude our friends, our spouses, or our bosses by causing them to think that their pleasure is our ultimate goal. You and the one you would please are not the only two beings in view—there is always God to consider.

This does not mean that God's laws don't matter. We have no liberty to lay them aside. But we do have liberty to lay aside the use of things God has approved. (We can never rightly take or use those things God has forbidden, and we must take or use those things God commands us to take or use.) But in that great category of liberty, those things that we *may* do, that are "permissible," as the Corinthians put it, those things we should sometimes lay aside whenever the good of another calls for it. Such love guiding the use of our liberties is the way of Christ, and so it glorifies God.

Look at how Paul closes this section of the letter with an exhortation: "Follow my example, as I follow the example of Christ" (11:1). Follow my example, he writes. Paul tries to be like Christ in this matter of living in love, and the Corinthians should, too. Paul practices what he preaches. Christ our sacrifice is also our example. I wonder what kind of examples you see around you? We should follow them only as they lead us to Christ, and *never* when they lead us away from him.

In all of this concern about how we behave, we must remember that Christians are not to be legalists. We have been liberated to follow Christ. We have our liberty, and we curtail it not out of legalism, but out of love—love for our fellow Christian or for the non-Christian with us. Ultimately, we curtail it out of our love for God.

Johann Sebastian Bach, a devout evangelical believer, used to sign his works, "S.D.G," from the Latin Vulgate phrase found in Romans 16:27: *Soli Deo Gloria*—"to the only God be glory." This became Bach's motto. He signed his works—whether sacred, such as "The St. Matthew Passion," or secular, such as the lighthearted "Coffee Cantata," with the letters S.D.G. *All* works, he maintained, should be to the glory of God. And that included the rearing of his family. Bach was a happily married, faithful husband and father. By his first wife, Barbara, he fathered three children. A year and a half after her death he married again and had seventeen more children by his second wife—all to the glory of God.

Friends, why do you think Christ gave himself for us? To save us? Yes; but why did he do that? Because of his love? Yes; but even his love for us is ultimately for the glory of God alone. Oh, my Christian brothers and sisters, meditate on what God has done in Christ. Soak yourself in his self-giving love. Put yourself around Christians who live like Christ—giving themselves in love for the good of others. What about your own example: are you a good model for others to follow? How are you not leading others to be like Christ? Are you being deliberate about loving others, trying to serve them as a good model?

In our churches, we must encourage individual discipling, working to help one another to help others. To that end, we must keep the gospel of Jesus Christ and his cross work for us at the center of our fellowship. We must gather to talk, to come to know one another so we can all live to glorify God even more. Flee from idols but embrace the true God. Live for him. Live for the true God's glory.

Conclusion

America continues to reflect on the life of Rosa Parks, even after her death in 2005. Much has been made of Mrs. Parks's action. In the language of the 1950s crusaders, her action did much to lift up a "downtrodden race." We don't really talk that way anymore. Today we speak more about how she made us a better nation. More equal and free. But what about Paul's teaching in 1 Corinthians? It seems to suggest that Mrs. Parks should simply have given up her seat for someone else, sacrificing her rights for the good of the other person.

From my Christian perspective, it is clear to me that Mrs. Parks, a deaconess in her church, by her refusal to move helped our brothers and sisters in Christ. She certainly helped our black brothers and sisters. But I think she helped even more her Christian brothers and sisters who were in the majority culture. All Christians, regardless of race, are used to suffering. We often have to endure it in a fallen world. But for Christians to inflict unjust suffering on others—including their brothers and sisters in Christ—this is something far worse. It stains our souls, and even worse, it lies about Jesus to the world. It was in this way—by showing us what we were doing—that Mrs. Parks's refusal to move served white Christians. She showed us how we were wrongly inflicting suffering on others. And so, though she helped black Christians in America, she has helped those of us who are white infinitely more in revealing to us our lack of love, and from that revelation flows conviction and change.

We should live not to abuse others but to bless others. Paul laid aside his right to financial support and to eat meat sacrificed to idols because of his love for the Corinthians, whether Jews or Gentiles, believers or unbelievers. And Christ, well, Christ laid aside his liberties of unbroken fellowship with the Father, of sinlessness, and even of life to effect his design of love in the lives of all those who would repent of their sins and trust in him. Christ is the great example of acting self-sacrificially in love for others. We do see Christ's love reflected in others. We see that love in the example of Paul and perhaps in Rosa Parks. Maybe you can see it in the lives of those around you. I pray that others will see Christ's example of self-sacrificial love in your life and in mine.

Forgoing your rights out of love for others is a Christlike thing to do, because through your actions God's glory appears, as people get even the tiniest glimpse of Jesus. It is that picture of God's love in Christ that we, as individuals and in our churches, want to display, because God is like that to us in Christ. We want to show others the gospel, even as we tell it to them, because doing so manifests and displays God's glory.

That is why Christians live lives of love—love toward others and ultimately love toward God. Are you living a life of love? I wonder why.

8

AUTONOMY

1 CORINTHIANS 11:2–16

Imagine visiting a church some Sunday, and upon entering you find the women dressed suggestively and the men giving you leering looks. As you settle in for the service, you overhear cryptic phrases and see a few hurried salutes suggesting a little bit more might be going on here than merely a *religious* meeting. It feels more like a political meeting, even a *subversive* one. As the service—the meeting—begins, you see that it is being led by a forceful woman whose words center around redefining marriage and sexuality. Did you hear right? Did she really suggest that a wife should be sexually active with people other than her husband? At this point, you become a little more than vaguely uncomfortable.

Afterward, as people are leaving the service, you can't help but notice signs of conspicuous wealth, at least on the part of a few people, and the wealthy ones are receiving a lot of deferential attention. As you leave, you realize that you heard and saw very little of anything that reflects the Christianity of the Bible. Come to think of it, mentions of Jesus weren't very clear, and they didn't use Bibles.

This is a picture of what I think Paul feared the Corinthian church was becoming, which is why he addresses several related issues in the passage before us now. First Corinthians 11:2–16 is a famously difficult passage, but in it many important questions are dealt with:

- In a Christian church, does it matter much what those outside of the church think of us? Does it matter what relationships between genders are like, especially in marriages?
- Does it matter how we understand God, and the relation of the Father to the Son?
- Does it matter how we as a Christian congregation regard the Bible or relate to other churches?
- Is being a Christian just about Jesus and me—regardless of my morality, my desires, my reputation, and my interests?

We want to think here about the inadequacy of autonomy—literally, self-law—as a way to understand following Christ, and we want to notice particularly the relationships that are to be considered as part of Christian discipleship. For most of this chapter, we will consider the relationship of Christians to one another and to unbelievers.

The Christian and Relationships

What we find in this portion of Paul's epistle is that Christians are not autonomous (vv. 4–7, 10, 13–15). This truth comes to the fore in Paul's comments about the Corinthians' gatherings. He was concerned that they were in danger of communicating all the wrong things to each other, and even to non-Christians who might naturally see their gatherings and wander in, whether from curiosity or less charitable reasons.

Reflecting on Paul's instructions here, we see that our desire and aim should be to communicate to each other, and especially to visitors, at least five things in our meetings: morality, authority, gender distinction, the gospel, and humility.

Morality

In our gatherings as believers we want to communicate that Christians are committed to holiness and righteousness and faithfulness in all our actions and relationships. That is the context in which we can best understand

Paul's desire here that women who pray or prophesy in the assembly have their heads covered:

> Every woman who prays or prophesies with her head uncovered dishonors her head—it is just as though her head were shaved. If a woman does not cover her head, she should have her hair cut off; and if it is a disgrace for a woman to have her hair cut or shaved off, she should cover her head. A man ought not to cover his head, since he is the image and glory of God; but the woman is the glory of man. For man did not come from woman, but woman from man; neither was man created for woman, but woman for man. For this reason, and because of the angels, the woman ought to have a sign of authority on her head. . . . Judge for yourselves: Is it proper for a woman to pray to God with her head uncovered? Does not the very nature of things teach you that if a man has long hair, it is a disgrace to him, but that if a woman has long hair, it is her glory? For long hair is given to her as a covering. (vv. 5–10, 13–15)

Paul teaches that long hair is given to a woman as her covering and her glory, i.e., that which adds luster to her. Specifically, in this case of long hair, you could say that a woman's hair reflects tenderness, softness, and beauty. That is the traditional view, the one held by the Corinthians—and most of the ancient Greeks and Romans. Therefore, it was a shock when, during these very years, a movement arose among women in Rome and in cities around the empire in which women were rejecting the use of head coverings in public. Women discarded their head coverings to indicate that they wanted to be treated equally to their husbands, particularly in the area of sexual liberties. Most pagans seemed to think little of a man having a number of different women to please him sexually, but such liberties, if taken by a woman, were scandalous.

Paul was concerned that some of what he may have been hearing was indicative that this cultural movement was making inroads at the church at Corinth. Such sexual license was in truth unfaithfulness, whether on the part of the husband or the wife. The infiltration of the movement into the Corinthian church may have been why the Corinthian Christians were allowing a woman to have sex with her stepson, a situation Paul addressed in chapter 5.

The growing movement is one reason that Paul is so insistent that the women should not be uncovered in public when they prayed. Paul taught them that man is symbolically dishonored when a woman prays with her head uncovered. Observers might think that the woman praying with uncovered head was doing so to proclaim her unfaithfulness to her husband.

A woman praying with her head uncovered dishonored her man because, at least according to widespread local custom, it suggested that she was not under her husband's authority. Headgear and hairstyle reflected one's status or situation in those days. A decision to remove the marriage veil in public would today be the cultural equivalent of you removing your wedding ring. Loose and flowing hair in Paul's day was associated with loose women, and even with the priestesses of pagan cults.

Some people have wondered if these verses refer only to married men and women, or if they refer to all men and women. The Greek words Paul used meant "men" and "women," but they also meant "husband" and "wife," which provides linguistic testimony to the normalcy of marriage in that culture. I think that these verses were written with husbands and wives uppermost in Paul's mind.

Paul implies that so long as coverings were worn, it was appropriate for women to pray or prophesy, just as Miriam prophesied in Exodus (15:20), Deborah in Judges (4:4), Mary in Luke (1:48), and the four daughters of Philip in Acts (21:9). This is why we will often have women praying publicly at our church prayer meeting on Sunday nights. But whatever these women were doing, it is clearly not the same as the "speaking in the churches," which, in 14:34, Paul says he does *not* allow. Additionally, women were not allowed to have authority over men, something Paul explicitly forbids in 1 Timothy 2:12. Women, therefore, were not to serve as elders.

Whenever a woman prayed in a public meeting, it is clear from Paul's words here in 1 Corinthians 11 that she should cover her head. If she didn't want to be shorn, then she should be veiled while praying in public for the honor of her husband. Paul's words were directed primarily to married women, although single women also were not to give the appearance of immorality. An unveiled woman accompanying a man in public signaled that she might not be his wife but rather a paid escort. "Judge for yourselves," Paul writes. "Is it proper for a woman [wife] to pray to God with her head uncovered?" Paul's clear implication is "you *know* that it's improper for a woman to pray with head uncovered." It makes her look like a sexually promiscuous woman.

A very odd aspect of Christianity to many today is our understanding that sexual pleasure is not harmless. Sex either helps unite you to your spouse or it does great harm. We understand Jesus Christ to be perfectly holy, and he calls us to be his people. That's why we Christians desire to encourage others to be moral. We don't want to dress or act in such a way as to present ourselves as objects of sexual desire to anyone other than our spouse. Christians, we must work to be faithful in our marriages and to be seen as faithful if we are going to be the people God is calling us to be. As we gather within our congregations, let us pray that our morality should distinguish us for God's glory. God's glory is why we have a church covenant and why we teach what we do. We stress membership, accountability, and even church discipline, because we understand that one role of the church is to communicate God's call to morally pure lives.

Authority

Another thing we want to communicate to one another in church and to those who visit our churches is an appreciation for authority. Respect for authority is another concern underlying Paul's teaching that women should be covered if they stand to lead in prayer in the public gathering.

One of the strangest parts of this challenging passage is Paul's argument in verse 10: "For this reason, and because of the angels, the woman ought to have a sign of authority on her head." Paul has concluded that a woman ought to have her head covered as a symbol of being under authority, but what do angels have to do with that? Many people have pointed out that these heavenly messengers are clearly present at our public services of worship. We know from the Old Testament that angels express submission to God by covering themselves in his presence (cf. Ex. 37:9; Isa. 6:2; Ezek. 1:11, 24), so maybe Paul presents the angels here as a model for the women to follow.

Others take this to mean that women ought to cover their heads in order not to shame themselves before the angels who would be witnessing their public worship. Still others have suggested that this is a reference to Old Testament law, which, according to tradition, had been given through angels. Maybe Paul's words were a reference to the authority established in Genesis at the creation of man, with woman as his helpmeet. Any of these could be true. But even if we do not understand why the angels are a motivation for this kind of action, the action itself is clear enough.

I was helped in my own understanding when I considered that the word translated "angels" simply means messengers. In Luke 7, for example, we read that when John the Baptist wondered whether Jesus was the Messiah, he sent some men to see Jesus and question him. Luke described these men as "messengers," using the same word that Paul uses here. Of course, the messengers in Luke were not heavenly beings; they were human scouts, messengers, sent out by John the Baptist. Therefore, I think it is quite possible that here in 1 Corinthians 11 Paul uses "messengers" to refer to human scouts sent from the city leaders, *from the authorities*.

The city leaders, these authorities, may have been interested in such meetings because they were so unusual. In the Roman world meetings or associations of this sort were allowed to gather only monthly or even less frequently. The Romans, remember, were military tyrants; they ruled by occupation, and rebellion was a constant problem. Therefore, their pacification plan included limiting the ability of people to assemble freely, openly, and regularly.

There was little religious pressure for exceptions to such a policy. Except for the great feasts, pagan worship was not tied to any kind of public meeting. There were no weekly gatherings. One just went by the temple at any time and gave an offering privately. The Jews were the only exception, and they had been granted a special legal exemption in order to meet weekly. At this point, the Christians were still considered a sect of the Jews.

We can see why the authorities might have had an interest in checking in on such meetings, especially if the meetings were marked by women speaking about socially disruptive ideas. The authorities would be interested indeed. Rebellion was a serious matter. Seditious gatherings could result in withdrawal of privileges from the entire city.

A woman's head covering communicated that she was under the authority of her husband, much like we use caps in the military. The head covering, like the military cap, was a sign on the highest part of the body, a sign of being under the authority of someone else. Paul was concerned that women not be uncovered so as to suggest disrespect toward authority.

It is hard for us today to hear of authority without immediately thinking of a negative authoritarianism, but surely we regularly experience the blessing of being under good authority. Though authority can be abused, Christians realize that authority is a good thing. We have seen such respect for authority in Jesus Christ, who always did his Father's will, and those of us who are Christians have experienced his kind rule in our lives.

So in your life, Christian wife, you want to work to submit to your husband. Christian child, you want to work to submit to your parents. Christian employee, you want to work to submit to your employers. As a congregation, we want to work to submit to the elders. We want to participate in meetings. We want to rejoice in each other, benefit from each other, and realize what a powerful witness a community working together is. Nothing in our meetings should undermine our evident respect for due authority.

Gender Distinctions

A third thing we want to communicate at our gatherings is an appreciation for gender distinctions. While it was culturally normal for women to be veiled in public, Paul stresses that men should not be covered: "Every man who prays or prophesies with his head covered dishonors his head" (v. 4). The head that gets dishonored is Christ, as Paul made clear in verse 3. So Christ was symbolically dishonored if a man prayed with his head covered.

One point of this passage is to display publicly appropriate gender-distinctive dress. God has revealed something of himself and his nature and character in the interrelation of two distinct genders, and the church is not to undermine or confuse that but to be an example of it. "A man ought not to cover his head, since he is the image and glory of God; but the woman is the glory of man" (v. 7). A man should not cover his head, because he, especially, is the glory of God, and covering his head would somehow dishonor God, while the woman is the glory of man. "A wife of noble character is her husband's crown" (Prov. 12:4).

One aspect of God's image especially displayed in the man is his *ruling*, whereas an aspect of God's image in the woman is *submitting*, as Christ did in the incarnation. Another aspect seen here of God's image reflected in men and women is his personal and relational nature. Even as fallen beings, we humans fulfill these roles. When Paul says that man is the glory of God and the woman is the glory of man, he is not denying that women are made equally in the image of God (cf. Gen. 1:27) and are also God's glory; rather, his words simply provide the additional information that women are also the glory of their husband. *Glory* is the reflection and revelation of the nature of a thing.

None of this suggests that a man has more ability than his wife but simply that there are roles that we are called to fulfill, roles that God has generally fitted us for, in order to show the excellence of God, his character, his creation, and, ultimately, his gospel. Faithful, loving leadership and trusting, joyful submission profoundly reflect the truth about God, us, and his gospel.

Verse 14 has caused great confusion. "Does not the very nature of things teach you that if a man has long hair, it is a disgrace to him?" Nature teaches us that it is disgraceful for a man to have long hair. There is very little in the Bible about hair length. Nazirites had long hair; priests did not. Absalom had it, but he didn't do well by it. Paul himself had had his hair cut off to keep a vow (Acts 18:18; cf. Acts 21:24), but other than these few references, we find nothing else.

So what does "nature" here refer to, and how does nature teach us the connection between honor and hair length? Men commonly lose their hair as they age, not due to any sort of disease but, rather, as part of the natural course of maturing. We know now that testosterone escalates hair loss. Estrogen, on the other hand, causes hair to grow longer; women usually do not go bald. So Paul might have meant that kind of physiological "nature."

Most commentators, however, think that Paul was referring more to common practice of the time. Greek cultures generally viewed long hair on a man as effeminate. One classical author referred to the long hair of an adolescent boy as "long girlish locks."[1] So for adult males to walk around Corinth with long hair gave the impression of a homosexual orientation.

In all of this, what Paul wanted the Corinthians—and us—to see is that gender distinctions are an innate part of human physiology and social norms, even if the specifics of the norms have some variations. Gender is not finally a social construction. It is God's idea, and it is not inherently oppressive. Your freedom, whether male or female, is found in your Creator's purpose for you. And he is a sure guarantor of your good, if you will entrust yourself to him.

As a Christian you might ask what you can do in this gender-hostile age to call attention to and celebrate God's wonderful creation of humanity as male and female. In our congregations, we must be faithful to God's displaying his image in male and female. We must follow through on distinctions in roles in the congregation that are clear in Scripture, even if they are unpopular in the world at large. We understand the Bible to teach that elders are to be men, that men are to marry only women, and women are to marry only men. We are called to be good models of each gender, complementing the other. We must communicate in our gatherings an appreciation for gender distinctions as well as the fact that God has designed us to reveal something of himself in how the distinctions work together.

The Gospel

The fourth thing that Paul desired the Corinthian congregation to communicate, and that we should want to communicate as well, is the gospel. Paul did not want the church misrepresenting the gospel, which is one reason he did not want the women to be uncovered. Gathering for worship dressed inappropriately would miscommunicate the gospel to all in sight. I think that this is one of Paul's primary motives for being so strong on this point. Just think of the danger of losing the gospel message in Corinth! The community at Corinth already viewed the Christians as strange for not having a statue to worship and for meeting publicly with such frequency. We recall that pagan worship was largely individual, except for public feasts, and, of course, a woman in the congregation had already committed adultery with her stepson. So if the growing cultural practice of uncovered women praying in public was adopted, Christianity's teaching on marriage would be hugely distorted in the eyes of the community. And Paul didn't want that.

Today we do not want to deceive unbelievers about the good news of Jesus Christ, which is that God has made us to know him and to reflect his image and character, but we have sinned against him. We have stored up against ourselves God's rightful wrath for our sins, wrath that would justly take us down to hell were it not for the amazing love of God that has come to us in Jesus Christ. God, the Son, took on flesh, became truly human, lived a perfect life, and was crucified, bearing God's wrath for our sins—the sins of all who will repent and trust in him. God raised Christ to life, in victory over sin and death. If we repent of our sins and trust in Christ, then we will be saved from the punishment due to us for our sins, from our self-enslavement to sin, and one day even from the very presence of sin itself, and we will come to spend eternity with God. Christ became our sacrifice.

My Christian friend, know the gospel. Share the gospel. Bring attention to the gospel by your life. Pray that your congregation will keep the gospel the main thing. In every sermon we want to relish God's bringing himself near to us by means of the gospel. We want to encourage each other with the gospel and pray that God will train our hearts to feed on it increasingly. The Corinthian church—and our church—should communicate the gospel.

Humility

A fifth thing we should communicate in our worship gatherings is humility. There is a connection between humility and Paul's teaching about head coverings, even though we do not see it from a direct reading of the passage. When Paul exhorts the men to pray with their heads uncovered, he is guiding them away from what was done elsewhere in Corinth. Social status in Corinth was indicated by dress, and the most wealthy and respected men, the priests, would pull over their heads a portion of their best toga when leading prayer in the pagan temples and at the great public feasts. Apparently some men in the congregation at Corinth were emulating this, but Paul attacked the practice because he desired humility rather than arrogance to be evident in the Christian assembly.

If we are honest, we must admit that today many people do not think of evangelical Christians as humble, because we are not. We are too focused on ourselves and too pleased with our own accomplishments. Conversely, Christians are judged as arrogant simply because they exhibit certainty in their Christian beliefs. As heralds of the gospel, we are condemned as arrogant in the mind of the society. As long as we testify solely about our own experience, we are fine. But the moment we move away from a subjective stance to one that is true for everyone, we are dismissed as proud, self-righteous, holier-than-thou know-it-alls. G. K. Chesterton summed up the situation well one hundred years ago:

> What we suffer from today is humility in the wrong place. Modesty has moved from the organ of ambition . . . [and] settled upon the organ of conviction, where it was never meant to be. A man was meant to be doubtful about himself, but undoubting about the truth; this has been exactly reversed. We are on the road to producing a race of men too mentally modest to believe in the multiplication table.[2]

The result of all this, brothers and sisters, is that we have to work all the harder at being humble in the right way. Appreciate Christ's humility. Read in Philippians 2 about Christ humbling himself to death, even death on the cross. Study the cross.

The last place in which money or other kinds of worldly status should be recognized is in a community of hell-deserving, blood-bought, grace-saved, Spirit-born sinners. Pray for your pastor's humility and that of the elders in your congregation. Pray that your church as a whole will exhibit humility as you read God's Word and are instructed and corrected by it. I pray that we all come to the same kind of humbling self-knowledge that D. L. Moody had when he said, "I have more problems with D. L. Moody than any other man I know."

Friends, humility is attractive, even compelling, and that is probably in no small part because it is so near an approximation of Christ's whole ministry. Our congregations must communicate humility. In sum, churches today are challenged to communicate—both to those within its walls and to those outside—morality, authority, gender distinctions, the gospel, and humility.

Husband and Wife

In 1 Corinthians 11 Paul gives special attention to the relationship between husband and wife, and one of the things we find in his words is that we are not autonomous in our homes. Paul tells the Corinthians that there is both a hierarchy and a mutuality that they are to experience and express in their marriages.

Hierarchy

"Man did not come from woman, but woman from man; neither was man created for woman, but woman for man" (vv. 8–9). That is God's plan. And if we are Christians, that is how we should understand marriage. This picture of marriage is rooted in the story of creation found in Genesis 1 and 2. There we learn how and why God created us male and female. This is why Paul instructs the Corinthian Christians as he does here, because of the order of creation: woman (Eve) was first created from man (Adam). In verse 9 Paul gives a second piece of the argument as to why the woman is the glory of the man: woman was made for man, not man for woman. Again, he is referring to the biblical teaching of God's creation of the world.

Many take this teaching as denigrating to women. While it can be abused that way, the task of *helping* is a wonderful reflection of the character and glory of God. Christianity has long been a force for society's respecting women. We have not been inveterate opponents of hierarchy. After all, we understand and believe in a Trinitarian God—Father, Son and Holy Spirit. The Son is a faithful Son who always does the Father's will, yet this in no way denigrates him or his dignity.

Wives, how have you helped your husband this week? Husbands, how have you led your wife? Have you taken any initiative to care for her or bless her or to do something for her good as one of your most important stewardships?

A commitment to complementarian teaching is a challenge for churches today, the position that men and women have distinct roles, but roles that are complementary and so bless and encourage one another.

Mutuality

Because men might easily distort the teaching Paul was giving here, he adds, "In the Lord, however, woman is not independent of man, nor is man independent of woman. For as woman came from man, so also man is born of woman. But everything comes from God" (vv. 11–12). Paul is saying that God is the author of all, and that men and women need each other. In Christ, men and women depend on each other; we are interdependent. We are to bear one another's burdens, especially in marriage. God has woven a beautiful interdependence between his people. We find it in friendships when we help each other, sometimes despite—many times because of and with—our very differences, and certainly in marriage.

In this letter Paul makes revolutionary statements regarding the role of women. Earlier we read, "The wife's body does not belong to her alone but also to her husband. In the same way, the husband's body does not belong to him alone but also to his wife" (7:4). Commentators say that there is no other teaching in antiquity quite like it, this claim that the husband's body belongs to the wife. In fact, it was inequity between men and women that had, in part, led to the women's movement among Roman wives that I mentioned earlier.

When Paul says that not only did woman come from man, but now all men come through women, and, of course, we all come from God, he is trying to make sure that husbands do not lord their authority over their wives. The Bible is clear in presenting not only the good wife as praiseworthy, but also the good husband as praising. In Proverbs 31 we read a paean to the noble wife: "A wife of noble character who can find? She is worth far more than rubies. . . . Her children arise and call her blessed; her husband also, and he praises her: 'Many women do noble things, but you surpass them all'" (Prov. 31:10, 28–29). Likewise, the apostle Peter calls husbands to be considerate of their wives (1 Pet. 3:7). So the relation of the genders, according to the Bible, includes both hierarchy and mutuality.

Cultures swing back and forth in their emphases, stressing either hierarchy or mutuality. Christian congregations have always been refuges from a wrong egalitarianism on the one hand and an exploitation and oppression on the other. For those who are single, this call to mutuality should encourage you to relate to each other as brothers and sisters for your mutual benefit. In our congregations, we want to encourage both men and women to grow in the Lord. We want to be committed to holding each other accountable for our relationships, including our marriages, because we understand this is part of following Jesus.

The Relationship of God the Father and God the Son

The relationship that lies at the core of biblical thinking about gender is one that may surprise some of you—the relationship between the Father and the Son. "Now I want you to realize that the head of every man is Christ, and the head of the woman is man, and the head of Christ is God," Paul writes (v. 3; cf. Eph. 1:22; 4:15; 5:23; Col. 1:18; 2:10, 19). We see that even Jesus was not autonomous. Understanding the relational aspects of the Trinity gives us insights into understanding gender roles. In Jesus' relationship to his Father, there is both equality and distinction. Looked at the other way, our understanding and experience of gender roles is an important way for us to come to understand God better. Paul actually begins this whole discussion by teaching the Corinthians that God is the head of Christ, who is the head of man, who is the head of woman.

This idea of *head* has always been present in the Bible's names for God. In the Old Testament we read, "Yours, O Lord, is the kingdom; you are exalted as head over all" (1 Chron. 29:11). The term is applied to Christ also (see Eph. 1:22; 4:15; 5:23; Col. 1:18; 2:10, 19). As Christ is head of all; the husband is head of the wife. *Headship* means "being over." In order to avoid the patriarchy in this language, "head" has sometimes been taken as "source of" rather than as "authority over." There are problems with this. First, there is no unambiguous use in Scripture of the Greek word *kefalh*, and, second, in the ancient world any such "source" would have had assumed authority, as naturally as parents do over children. We see this idea in English, such as in the word *author*, which is the basis for the word *authority*.

Paul is talking not about substances but about roles. While there is a substantial difference between Christ and men, there is no such difference of *substance* between either God and Christ or men and women. God the Father and God the Son are equal in personhood and importance (John 10:30; 17:21–24). So, too, are men and women. At the same time, there is a difference in *roles* between God the Father and God the Son (see 1 Cor. 3:23; 15:27–28; cf. John 4:34; 5:30; 6:38) and between husband and wife.

Both men and women are fully human, made in the image of God. Paul says in Galatians 3:28 that there is no male or female, not, of course, in relation to physical gender or in the roles we are called to fulfill, but simply in regard to our status before God. Whether lost or saved, we are truly and fully human. Wayne Grudem writes on this point:

Paul is here underlining the fact that no class of people, such as the Jewish people who had come from Abraham by physical descent, or the freedmen who had greater economic and legal power, could claim special status or privilege in the church. Slaves should not think themselves inferior to free men or women, nor should the free think themselves superior to slaves. Jews should not think themselves superior to Greeks, nor should Greeks think themselves inferior to Jews. Similarly, Paul wants to insure that men will not adopt some of the attitudes of the surrounding culture, or even some of the attitudes of first-century Judaism, and think that they have greater importance than women or are of superior value before God. Nor should women think themselves inferior or less important in the church. Both men and women, Jews and Greeks, slaves and free, are equal in importance and value to God and equal in membership in Christ's body, the church, for all eternity.[3]

Relationships within the Church

We conclude by looking at relationships within the church, which is important because we are not autonomous as a congregation. The first important aspect of such relationships is a submission to apostolic teaching.

Submission to Apostolic Teaching

Paul writes, "I praise you for remembering me in everything and for holding to the teachings, just as I passed them on to you" (v. 2). Paul is referring to teaching that is apostolic, and he commends the Corinthians for holding to it. Once again we see Paul commenting on evidences of grace, just as he had at the beginning of the letter. He may, in part, be offering a word of reassurance after his very strong words of correction in the last few chapters. Such assurance would also serve to encourage them to obey the instruction he is about to give them. For us today, all this means that we must know the Word; we must give ourselves to studying and obeying it.

Respect for Other Churches

There is another relationship that Paul encourages the congregation to be conscious of as a guide and safeguard, and that is the one each congregation has with other churches. "If anyone wants to be contentious about this, we have no other practice—nor do the churches of God" (v. 16). In other words, the apostolic teaching is universal and therefore allows for no division over it. We do no wrong in seeking to get our bearings, at least partially, from the practice of other congregations. *New* and *improved* are great words to use in advertising copy but not normally in Christianity, which does not get new and improved.

Of course, not all customs are good, which is why Paul earlier criticized the *practice* of idolatry (8:7), using the same word there as he does here in verse 16. Idolatry is a practice that is clearly forbidden throughout the Bible. Paul makes clear that those in the congregation who are contentious, literally "victory lovers," contradict this practice.

Conclusion

In our lost and confused day, may we, in our congregations, exemplify morality and authority and appreciation of the wonderful genders God has given us. May we be faithful in presenting the gospel of Jesus Christ and in exemplifying it in humility, especially in our marriages, as we lead and help and as we value each other. And in all of this may we be a revelation of God and his character to the world around us.

9

THOUGHTLESSNESS

1 CORINTHIANS 11:17—34

What, to the American slave, is your Fourth of July? I answer; a day that reveals to him, more than all other days in the year, the gross injustice and cruelty to which he is the constant victim. . . . You boast of your love of liberty, your superior civilization and your pure Christianity, while the whole political power of the nation . . . is solemnly pledged to support and perpetuate the enslavement of three millions of your countrymen. . . . You can bare your bosom to the storm of British artillery to throw off a three-penny tax on tea; and yet wring the last hard-earned farthing from the grasp of the black laborers of your country. You profess to believe "that, of one blood, God made all nations of men to dwell on the face of all the earth" [Acts 17:26], and hath commanded all men, everywhere, to love one another; yet you notoriously hate (and glory in your hatred) all men whose skins are not colored like your own. . . . The existence of slavery in this country brands your republicanism as a sham, your humanity as a base pretense, and your Christianity as a lie.

That was Frederick Douglass's famous speech on Independence Day, 1852, in an address to the Ladies' Anti-Slavery Society of Rochester, New York.[1] In these remarks, Douglass charged Christian slaveholders with hypocrisy. He was, in a different way, calling all Americans hypocrites who claimed to believe in the goodness and rightness of the Bill of Rights and of their country. His criticisms were faithful; sin had to be called out. Douglass functioned as a secular prophet.

We do not like being called hypocrites. It presumes that others know more about who we are than we may know ourselves. They know who they say we are, they know who we really are, and they know the two are different. And they say so. Can Christians ever be marked by such hypocrisy? What, at the very core, would render Christians hypocritical?

In Corinth there existed a sort of hypocritical, self-serving religious thinking, and the hypocrisy was one of the challenges that Paul addressed in his first epistle to the church in Corinth. There was such thoughtlessness among the believers there that their profession of faith in Christ was becoming obscured.

Let me recap the context in which Paul's letter is set. Paul had planted the church there and had left it after staying there for a year and a half. Later, word had come to Paul about a number of problems in the church—various divisions, immorality, and a failure of love. In the passage we will examine in this chapter, we will learn three simple but related truths about thoughtlessness, selfishness, division and unity, and how they are related. Ultimately we will learn about how we must follow Christ together in his church.

Division in the Church

The first lesson we learn is that division in the church undermines its true identity. The divisions in the Corinthian church were raising questions about whether the church was truly Christian. Paul begins this section harshly, sounding more like he did back in chapters 4 to 6: "In the following directives I have no praise for you, for your meetings do more harm than good" (v. 17).

Paul had learned of a tragedy at his beloved Corinthian church—their very meetings were becoming harmful—when the whole purpose of having them was to build up and edify each member and to build up the church. Just a few verses earlier Paul had praised them for holding to the things that he had taught them, but now, he says, "I hear that your meetings are terrible—even destructive!"

He continues, "In the first place, I hear that when you come together as a church, there are divisions among you, and to some extent I believe it" (v. 18). That last phrase is probably better translated "and I believe the report of it." While I am sure he wished it were not true, he showed no doubt in the credibility of the report. Understand the sadness of this! How ironic that they were divided when they came together as a body. This is not what a church is to be like. Paul had already raised the issue of division back in 1:10–12, but now he returns to it. It seems the Corinthian congregation was reflecting more of the culture of Corinth than Paul would have liked. The church was acting like a secular ecclesia, divided over politics, status and wealth, and ethnicity. The believers were not acting like Christians should act.

Paul adds, "No doubt there have to be differences among you to show which of you have God's approval" (v. 19). Perhaps Paul was saying, sarcastically, "I guess divisions are necessary to show who is right!" Or he might have been merely observing the irony in the fact that their divisions were now necessary to show what in fact was truly right. Either way, Paul was reflecting on how sad it was that divisions were marking this congregation he loved so much.

Can you imagine how sad Paul must have been? He had seen this congregation born; he had loved and labored over it, and now he was watching its dissolution and demise. The divisions indicated something far worse than a mere lack of wisdom, as was the case with some of the earlier questions he dealt with about liberty. The divisions here evidenced a lack of love itself, a lack of love for one another, which suggested an even deeper lack of love—love for God. These divisions raised questions about whether this congregation was truly Christian.

All of this had come to a head in what Paul addresses next. He turns specifically to the Lord's Supper, and he says that their divisions demonstrated that the supper they were observing was not the Lord's. Paul was blunt. "When you come together, it is not the Lord's Supper you eat" (v. 20). I think Paul was simply saying that their divisions disqualify the supper they were having as being truly the Lord's Supper. So he says here, "At your gatherings, you're clearly not celebrating the *Lord's* Supper!"

He describes something of their celebrations in verse 21: "As you eat, each of you goes ahead without waiting for anybody else. One remains hungry, another gets drunk." Their suppers had become an orgy of *selfishness* rather than a feast of *sacrificial* love. Paul is suggesting to them that if they were really observing the Lord's Supper, they would be caring for each other in the way they chose to celebrate it. As it is, this rite that stood at the center of the church's life as a symbol of Christian unity became the very indicator of how un-Christian they were.

What exactly was going on here? The ancient Roman world at that time ran on a ten-day calendar, while the Jews (and therefore the Christians) ran on a seven-day calendar. The Christians were committed to meeting together each Sunday to correspond to the resurrection day of Christ. If they could not meet early in the morning, they would meet at night, and this seems to have been the case with the Corinthians. So the wealthy were able to show up well before others had gotten off work. Apparently the wealthy believers were sharing a meal together, others joining in as they arrived, leaving those who arrived last—those who had least control of their schedules and the least resources—perhaps to find nothing left from the fellowship meal that they had intended to share together before the Lord's Supper. Instead, the latecomers would find drunkenness. In short, it looked a lot like the secular private dinners and feasts in Corinthian culture. So the meal that was intended to build fellowship ended up only bonding some of them together while leaving others out. Their "table fellowship" before the Lord's Supper was causing division.

Now, consider how opposed to the nature of the church this was. Paul had already written to them, "Because there is one loaf, we who are many, are one body, for we all partake of the one loaf" (10:17). We are the fellowship of the loaf. We are one body. In fact, in the verse before that (10:16), we read, "Is not the cup of thanksgiving for which we give thanks a fellowship in the blood of Christ? And is not the bread that we break a fellowship in the body of Christ?" The church is a fellowship in the blood of Christ, the body of Christ. We are the fellowship of the body and blood of Christ.

But now Paul heard something bad was happening in his beloved Corinthian congregation, even as they gathered to celebrate the Lord's Supper. These were terrible divisions, and Paul is almost beside himself: "Don't you have homes to eat and drink in? Or do you despise the church of God and humiliate those who have nothing? What shall I say to you? Shall I praise you for this? Certainly not!" (v. 22). Their supper despised the church and humiliated the poor, whereas Christ cherished the church and gave himself for those who had nothing. And they were calling this the Lord's Supper!

The situation might have been heightened by a famine (perhaps the "crisis" Paul referred to back in 7:26), but whatever the situation, this is not how Christians were to deal with each other. This is, remember, the church of God, as Paul referred to these believers back at the beginning of the letter. It is God's church, not theirs.

Unbelievers may not understand why this is such a major issue, but we Christians, though we may do a poor job of it, are meant to exemplify self-sacrificial love for others because that's the love that Jesus has shown us. Christ is, as Paul says elsewhere, the head of the church. He is the one who directs us and guides us, and he has called us to follow his lead. His Spirit indwells us. We must realize that our actions affect others and, indeed, can affect the whole church. We sometimes forget this, but it is true. When we share something with someone, or fail to, when we care for someone, or fail to, when we include someone, or fail to, we affect the excluded one more than we probably realize. All our actions go toward building the culture of our congregation; our actions normalize behavior, whether for good or ill.

So how can we better reflect the character of Christ? We can be especially aware of selfishness, which causes divisions. There will be natural fault lines in any congregation—old and young, married and single, race, status—we want to be especially careful not to undermine these. We want to guard against harming other Christians but instead labor to help them. We must follow Christ's example and put others' needs before our own. I am helped by recalling the little mnemonic J.O.Y.—Jesus, others, you. We must work to make sure to build relationships with different types of people, others who aren't just like us, and to care about them and to let them care for us.

In our churches we must care for those in our number who are in financial and physical need. Christian love is real. In our life together as a body we should give ourselves to celebrating the Lord's Supper with genuine, joyful thanksgiving and a matching carefulness in order to reflect the sacrificial love we celebrate and even claim by this Supper. We must recognize and pray about threats to the unity of our congregation. We should cherish the unity that we have and work to protect it. We should encourage attendance at worship for all.

Their supper despised the church and humiliated the poor, whereas Christ cherished the church and *gave* himself for those who had nothing.

True Unity Is in Christ

The second point Paul makes in this section is that true unity is anchored in Christ. This is where congregations find their unity, where they nourish it, where they recover it. Christ's Supper points us to unity in Christ in at least four ways: (1) We remember Christ together by his Supper; we remember what Christ did. (2) We renew our covenant with Christ together by his Supper; we remember what we are doing. (3) We proclaim Christ's death together by his Supper; we will do what we pray. (4) We continue together feeding on Christ by faith until he returns; we think about what Christ will do.

Remembering Christ by His Supper

When we participate in the Supper as a unified congregation, we are re-membering Christ together. Paul tells the Corinthians what Christ had told his followers:

> For I received from the Lord what I also passed on to you: The Lord Jesus, on the night he was betrayed, took bread, and when he had given thanks, he broke it and said, "This is my body, which is for you; do this in remembrance of me." In the same way, after supper he took the cup saying, "This cup is the new covenant in my blood; do this, whenever you drink it, in remembrance of me" (vv. 23–26).

Paul knew Jesus' story and intended to follow Christ. Some today suggest that Paul was the founder of Christianity, but here is that most central of Christian observances, and Paul himself is concerned to remind the Corin-thians that it was Christ who had instituted it in his final days. The Last Supper is terribly important because of what Jesus teaches us through it about his death. Christ clearly instructed his followers to eat the bread in remembrance of him.

The Old Testament reveals that remembrance was a vital thing for the people of God. Remembering kept them encouraged in hard times; it kept before them their identity as God's people; it enabled them to pass along the truths of God to each generation; and remembering brought glory to God. Passover, of course, was the most significant covenantal remembrance and renewal in the life of Israel. Christ gave this meal, the Last Supper, to his followers so that the cross would be central.

That's why Christ instructed his followers to drink the cup in remem-brance of him. We can be quite sure that this vivid imagery would have been shocking to the Palestinian Jewish disciples of Jesus, yet such vivid imagery is typical of Jesus' teaching. The ratification of the old covenant was also by blood. A new covenant had been promised (Jer. 31:31)—a covenant that would fulfill God's promise of blessings to the nations (see Gen. 12:3). In his death Jesus fulfilled this covenant.

In the Old Testament we find imagery of the cup of God's wrath to be drunk by the wicked. We read: "In the hand of the LORD is a cup full of foaming wine mixed with spices; he pours it out, and all the wicked of the earth drink it down to its very dregs" (Ps. 75:8). Similarly, the prophet Isaiah said, "Awake, awake! Rise up, O Jerusalem, you who have drunk from the hand of the LORD the cup of his wrath, you who have drained to its dregs the goblet that makes men stagger" (Isa. 51:17). Jeremiah tells us, "This is what the LORD, the God of Israel, said to me: 'Take from my hand this cup filled with the wine of my wrath and make all the nations to whom I send you drink it. When they drink it, they will stagger and go mad because of the sword I will send among them'" (Jer. 25:15–16).

The evening on which Jesus established the Supper is also the occasion on which he predicts that he will be betrayed and killed. After the Supper, he goes to the garden of Gethsemane to pray, which he does as he considers his impending death:

> He fell with his face to the ground and prayed, "My Father, if it is possible, may this cup be taken from me. Yet not as I will, but as you will." . . . He went away a second time and prayed, "My Father, if it is not possible for this cup to be taken away unless I drink it, may your will be done." (Matt. 26:39, 42)

Jesus drank that bitter cup of God's wrath not because of his own sins; he drank it for others, for us, because of our sins. Christ's death, then, was a sacrifice for his followers. It was a new covenant, a new Passover, bringing redemption and starting the new covenant. It was the beginning of the kingdom of God on earth.

Oh, brothers and sisters, remember Christ. Meditate on the cost of God's forgiveness of your sins. Rejoice in God's loving provision. Praise God for how he uses his Supper to keep Christ and his death at the center of our life together in the church. Even in churches that have grown silent about the substitutionary, atoning death of Jesus Christ, the table is left as a telling and eloquent testimony to Christ's death and its benefits as the very center of Christian fellowship. Just as he designed it—we remember Christ together by his Supper.

We Renew Our Covenant

When we participate in the Supper as a congregation, we build unity by renewing our covenant with Christ. The new covenant established by Christ's death is recalled by observing his Supper and by the repeated observance of it. Our churches are called to reflect Christ's character corporately, so when we partake, we pledge to God, to each other, and to the world that we are participating in this covenant. We renew our covenant with Christ together by his Supper.

We Proclaim Christ's Death

When we participate in the Supper as a congregation, we are together proclaiming Christ's death. "For whenever you eat this bread and drink this cup, you proclaim the Lord's death until he comes" (v. 26). At the center of this meal is a message that many will find strange, but the message is what Christ's death is all about. Christ's death is our sacrifice that both satisfies the justice of God and accomplishes his purposes of mercy and love. We proclaim Christ's death by participating together in the Supper.

We Feed on Christ and Await His Coming

When we participate in the Supper as a unified congregation, we are feeding on Christ by faith, and we will do so until he returns. This supper also reminds us what Christ will do. "Whenever you eat this bread and drink this cup you proclaim the Lord's death until he comes." We are to continue doing this until Christ comes back. Do you know what that means? It means that you should come to Communion. If you call yourself a Christian, you should note when your church celebrates the Lord's Supper, and you should be there. Let me challenge you, brothers and sisters, come to the Lord's table; even if the distance is great from your home, your job is demanding, you are feeling down—whatever your reason might be—come to the Lord's table, as Christ has commanded all of those who call themselves his followers. When you come, come with a happy expectancy. We are not sharing a funeral meal together; we are having a dress rehearsal for the wedding supper of the Lamb. This One who was crucified as a criminal will return as our Judge and King. That is what this Supper is all about.

Unfortunately, in the Corinthian church their own meal was distorting Christ's Supper rather than allowing Christ's Supper to shape their meal. Christ's selfless love ends divisions in a truly Christian congregation. The Lord's Supper is where congregations find their unity, where they nourish it, where they recover it, not because of the Supper itself, but because of what it proclaims—Christ and his death.

Selfish Division Brings Judgment

The third lesson we learn from this section of the epistle is that selfish division in the church is sin and it brings God's judgment. The fact that the Corinthians were partaking of the Lord's Supper in an unworthy manner was indicative of serious problems within the church and among its members.

First, partaking of the Lord's Supper in an unworthy manner is sin: "Therefore, whoever eats the bread or drinks the cup of the Lord in an unworthy manner will be guilty of sinning against the body and blood of the Lord" (v. 27). Paul is saying that participating in this meal while being careless about sin in your life is to commit another sin against Christ. That's what I think Paul means by "an unworthy manner"; it is an adverbial phrase about how one is to approach the Lord's Supper. Paul is not condemning the unworthiness of the partaker—it is only unworthy people who may approach the Lord's table! "Worthy" people do not see their need of the Lord's Supper or what it symbolizes. Approaching the table in an unworthy manner is to do so acknowledging Christ's death and simultaneously harboring sin without contrition or self-examination.

The sin is not committed against the bread and wine, nor is it committed against the body of the church. While the church is referred to as the body of Christ, it is never referred to as his blood. Paul refers here to sinning against the body and blood of the Lord himself, the one who hung on the cross.

The Corinthians were approaching the Lord's Supper in an unworthy manner because they were being careless about sin, specifically, their treatment of each other. Paul wants them to understand that eating the bread or drinking the cup of the Lord in an unworthy manner is itself a sin. Brothers and sisters, consider the weightiness of sin. See the extent to which God will punish it. See the extent to which it would damn you. See the unremitting nature of its opposition to God. It was sin that first ran the knowledge of the love of God out of our hearts! It is sin that tells you that God is untrustworthy. It is sin that accuses God of lying. It is sin that tells you to trust in sin. Sin is terrible to you. It always has been and always will be. Unworthily partaking in the Lord's Supper is sin.

As we study Paul's words, we see that not only do we sin when we unworthily partake of the Lord's Supper, but doing so also brings about judgment: "For anyone who eats and drinks without recognizing the body eats and drinks judgment on himself" (v. 29). In other words, you do not want to take this meal if you do not recognize and appropriate the real fruits of Jesus' death in your own life.

This is what I think Paul means by the phrase "recognizing the body." I don't think he is referring to a recognition of the church as the body, although the expression of their sin is indeed harmful to the local congregation. Elsewhere in the letter Paul refers to the church as the body of Christ (see 6:15; 10:17; 12:12–13), but here he seems to be referring to Christ directly. If you partake of this meal without recognizing Jesus' life-giving rule in your life, then you are eating and drinking judgment on yourself.

This certainly does not mean that we should only come to the Lord's Supper when we are sinlessly perfect. As the hymn says, "If you tarry til you're better, you may never come at all." The focus of the Supper is Jesus and his righteousness for us, his having drunk the cup of the Father's wrath for us. We are not the focus of the Supper. To fail to recognize this is not only sin, but it will also bring judgment. Christ is the risen Judge. Brothers and sisters, acknowledge and profit from God's discipline in your life. Observe hard circumstances and see how God has blessed you through them and how you can use them well—for him and for his work in your life. Encourage your congregation to refrain from keeping sin secret; practice church discipline, as Paul urged back in chapter 7.

We see that unworthily partaking of the Lord's Supper is sin and that it brings judgment, but it also brings death: "That is why many among you are weak and sick, and a number of you have fallen asleep" (v. 30). This verse surprises people, but it should not. Paul is telling the Corinthians that some of the problems they were experiencing were actually God's judgment on them for continuing to live so contrarily to their profession of faith. The church is vitally important to God, and he will act to preserve it.

We cannot reason backward from an individual death to the sin that might have caused it, as we see in the trials of Job. But we do know that physical weakness and illness can be God's punishment. My non-Christian friend, you need to take note of this. It is clear in the Bible that sometimes, even in this life, God judges physically. Spiritual failure may be met by physical judgment, which is within the pale of what God has a right to do, and, in fact, has done. God did it with Ananias and Sapphira (Acts 5) and with Adam and Eve (Genesis 3), and, of course, with Jesus on our behalf.

Here in Corinthians Paul names one consequence of sin that he says is even worse than physical death: "When we are judged by the Lord, we are being disciplined so that we will not be condemned with the world" (v. 32). Unworthily partaking may lead to condemnation. God's judgment is his discipline to stop us from being condemned with the world. Such provisional judgments are part of God's goodness to us, and they often precede occasions of spiritual revival. God is stirring us, warning us, before it is too late. If we continue on in sin, then we will find that there are consequences to our actions and, ultimately, that God has established them. In the long run, our lives may show our profession of faith to be false.

Brothers and sisters, consider the fearfulness of God's wrath and condemnation. Scripture refers to a day to come that will be a day of wrath. If you know anything of the terror of hurricanes and tsunamis and tornados and earthquakes, then surely you realize that you do not want to see a day that could be well summarized with that one simple word—*wrath*.

How do we avoid such fearful condemnation? We know we can, because we see Paul pleading with the Corinthians to do so here in this passage: "A man ought to examine himself before he eats of the bread or drinks of the cup. . . . But if we judged ourselves, we would not come under judgment" (vv. 28, 31). So Paul tells the Corinthians: examine yourselves, judge yourselves.

All of this is why you want to examine yourself before you partake in Communion. It is important to reflect on your life. For the Corinthians, the partisan spirit and lack of compassion stood in obvious contradiction with what they were supposed to be celebrating, much like American liberty being celebrated by slaveholders. Would there be an obvious contradiction with you, if you were to approach the table today?

Paul says here that we will not be exposed to divine judgment if we are careful to examine ourselves before partaking. The Lord's Supper provides regular opportunity for spiritual and moral self-examination. Of course, we need to examine ourselves because we tend not to think about our sin. It has been said that if you asked a fish to describe its life, it probably would not mention the water because water is its natural environment. A fish just assumes water. That is a good picture of what we are like with our sins, which is why we all need to examine ourselves.

We must repent of our sins and trust in God's provision through the death of Christ. In our congregations we need to help each other. That is why churches ought to stress the importance of membership.

Also, we need to come to the Lord's Supper so that we can be, as the Second London Confession puts it, worthy receivers:

Worthy receivers, outwardly partaking of the visible Elements in this Ordinance, do then also inwardly by faith, really and indeed, yet not carnally, and corporally, but spiritually receive, and feed upon Christ crucified and all the benefits of his death: the Body and Blood of Christ, being then not corporally, or carnally, but spiritually present to the faith of Believers, in that Ordinance, as the Elements themselves are to their outward senses.

Selfish division in the church is sin against Christ, and it brings God's judgment.

Conclusion: Act in Love (11:33–34)

The sum of Paul's entire teaching here is that we are to act in love. "So then, my brothers, when you come together to eat, wait for each other. If anyone is hungry, he should eat at home, so that when you meet together it may not result in judgment. And when I come I will give further directions" (vv. 33–34). Be thoughtful, Paul instructs. Wait for each other. Be thoughtful for yourselves also, so that you will not be liable to God's judgment. Satisfy your hunger at home so you will not be tempted into actions that might bring about God's judgment.

My friends, we all struggle with selfishness. We are tempted—like the Corinthians—to seek our happiness at the expense of others. But we must resist. We must desire above all to please Christ, who died for us—so much so that we would even suffer and die for Christ in order that our joy might be fully in him. We must not be thoughtless hypocrites but rather loving Christians, good witnesses and saved sinners.

John Bunyan told of a day when he was tormented by thoughts of his hypocrisy, sin, and shortcomings:

Now while the Scriptures lay before me, and laid sin anew at my door, that saying in Luke xviii.1, with others, did encourage me to prayer; then the tempter again laid at me very sore, suggesting, "That neither the mercy of God, nor yet the blood of Christ, did at all concern me, nor could they help me for my sin; therefore it was but in vain to pray."

Yet, thought I, "I will pray."

"But," said the tempter, "your sin is unpardonable."

"Well," said I, "I will pray."

"It is to no boot," said he.

Yet, said I, "I will pray."

So I went to prayer with God; and while I was at prayer, I uttered words to this effect: "Lord, Satan tells me, that neither thy mercy, nor Christ's blood is sufficient to save my soul; Lord, shall I honour thee most, by believing thou wilt, and canst? or him, by believing that thou neither wilt, nor canst? Lord, I would fain honour thee, by believing that thou wilt, and canst."[2]

Honor Christ today by believing that his blood is sufficient to save your soul, and then turn and love others as Christ has loved you.

10

SELFISHNESS

1 CORINTHIANS 12–14

In 1917 *The Ladies Home Journal* listed ten reasons for going to church:

1. In the actual world, a churchless community—a community where men have abandoned and scoffed at or ignored their religious needs—is a community on the rapid downgrade.

2. Church work and church attendance mean the cultivation of the habit of feeling some responsibility for others and the sense of braced moral strength which prevents a relaxation of one's own moral fiber.

3. There are enough holidays for most of us which can quite properly be devoted to pure holiday making. Sundays differ from other holidays—among other ways—in the fact that there are 52 of them every year. . . . On Sunday, go to church.

4. Yes, I know all the excuses. I know that one can worship the Creator and dedicate oneself to good living in a grove of trees, or by a running

brook, or in one's own house. But I also know as a matter of cold fact the average man does not thus worship or thus dedicate himself. If he strays away from church he does not spend his time in good works or lofty meditation. He looks over the colored supplement of the newspaper.

5. He may not hear a good sermon at church. But unless he is very un- fortunate he will hear a sermon by a good man who, with his good wife, is engaged all the week long in a series of wearing, humdrum and important tasks for making hard lives a little easier.

6. He will listen to and take part in reading some beautiful passages from the Bible. And if he's not familiar with the Bible, he has suffered a loss.

7. He will probably take part in singing some good hymns.

8. He will meet and nod to, or speak to, good, quiet neighbors. . . . He will come away feeling a little more charitably toward all the world, even toward those excessively foolish young men who regard churchgoing as rather a soft performance.

9. I advocate a man's joining in church works for the sake of showing his faith by his works.

10. The man who does not in some way . . . connect himself with some active, working church misses many opportunities for helping his neighbors, and therefore, incidentally, for helping himself.

That was the president of the United States—not the current one, but the president from one hundred years ago, Teddy Roosevelt. Those were Teddy Roosevelt's ten reasons for going to church. Some of them are pretty good; we should assume all of them were well meant. Yet there is just a tinge of selfishness about the way the whole thing is presented; not selfishness in the Christian hedonist kind of way but in the saved-by-my-own-goodness kind of way. I am no expert on the former president or on his theology. I do know that one of his children remarked about him, "When father goes to a wedding, he wants to be the bride; when he goes to a funeral, he wants to be the corpse."[1] This kind of egotism and self-centeredness, which his children joked about, was routinely observed in Teddy Roosevelt. I read

Edmund Morris's two-volume biography on Roosevelt some time ago, and I was struck by many things but none more than this: Roosevelt's apparent complete absorption in whatever gripped his personal fancy. At its best, such intense absorption was a wonderful trait, enabling him to lose himself in a greater task. At its worst, it brought a tyrannically narrow perspective to all he surveyed. Such self-centeredness is typical of too much of today's thinking about Christianity, about being a Christian, and even about the church. It is also one way to summarize the problem that Paul was dealing with in the Corinthian church. Why do *you* go to church?

Throughout our study of 1 Corinthians, we have noticed something contrary—the theme of selflessness—running through the whole letter. In chapter 9 Paul defended the way he conducted his apostleship, using himself as an example of laying aside rights for the good of others. It was this same sort of selflessness that Paul enjoined the Corinthians to exercise in the matter of food sacrificed to idols in chapters 8 and 10. All of that falls under the general principle of acting for the good of others.

Another example of selflessness is the service of the true apostles that Paul described in the first four chapters of the epistle. There he recounted his selfless desires in being poured out for the edification of the whole rather than pursuing selfish ambitions and balkanizing the church, dividing it up for his own ends, as some in the Corinthian church seemed to be doing.

The principle of selflessness is threaded throughout Paul's discussion about church discipline in chapter 5, and in chapter 6 there is his willingness to be wronged; selflessness also undergirds his strong words on morality in chapters 6 and 7. Self-sacrificial consideration of others in conducting their worship services is Paul's exhortation to the Corinthians in chapters 11 and 14, and he gives the same exhortation in the use of their spiritual gifts in chapters 12 and 14, and in the concern for God's people elsewhere in chapter 16. Lastly, Paul's commitment to selflessness finds its core in the love described and enjoined in chapter 13.

As we study chapters 12 to 14 we are going to consider the challenge that selfishness brings to the church, and we will consider five defenses against selfishness that God has set up in his church: (1) order, (2) unity, (3) mutuality, (4) love, and (5) edification. Paul had been hearing about some selfish behaviors within the Corinthian church:

> If anyone speaks in a tongue, two—or at the most three—should speak, one at a time, and someone must interpret. If there is no interpreter, the speaker should keep quiet in the church and speak to himself and God. Two or three

prophets should speak, and the others should weigh carefully what is said. And if a revelation comes to someone who is sitting down, the first speaker should stop. For you can all prophesy in turn so that everyone may be instructed and encouraged. The spirits of prophets are subject to the control of prophets. For God is not a God of disorder but of peace. As in all the congregations of the saints, women should remain silent in the churches. They are not allowed to speak, but must be in submission, as the Law says. If they want to inquire about something, they should ask their own husbands at home; for it is disgraceful for a woman to speak in the church. Did the word of God originate with you? Or are you the only people it has reached? If anybody thinks he is a prophet or spiritually gifted, let him acknowledge that what I am writing to you is the Lord's command. If he ignores this, he himself will be ignored. Therefore, my brothers, be eager to prophesy, and do not forbid speaking in tongues. But everything should be done in a fitting and orderly way. (1 Cor. 14:27–40)

Order

One guard against selfishness that God has set in the church is order. He would have us undermine the effects of selfishness by being orderly. We can just picture what Paul was hearing: one coming into a church meeting and finding many people giving ecstatic messages in tongues, with few if any of these messages being interpreted. There were perhaps ten or fifteen prophecies—sermons or exhortations of various lengths—sometimes a second one starting up before the first one was even done. The voices of women mixed with those of the men, perhaps yelling out about whether this prophecy or that should be regarded as valid—and this in a culture where women never spoke in secular assemblies! This describes the situation that Paul had heard of in the public meetings of the Corinthian church, so Paul, by means of this letter, walks in and restores order. The meeting, he says, should reflect God's character. "God is not a God of disorder but of peace" (v. 33).

Paul tells the congregation that the tongues speakers should be limited in the meeting. Do not be intimidated by their ecstasy, he warns. Furthermore, if there is no interpreter, tongues should not be spoken at all. Paul is getting quite specific here about his instructions for public worship. He is concerned that the gospel may be gaining a bad name in Corinth because of the disorder in the meetings of the Corinthian church. The messages should be limited and interpreted, and even then, only two or three ought to be allowed.

Even prophets should be limited in the meeting, and they, too, must be evaluated. Paul clearly expected that more than one person might be led by God's Spirit to speak at a church meeting, although not everyone would be so led because, as Paul points out (12:29), not everyone is given the gift of prophecy. Here he clearly limits those who will speak to two or three per meeting. We do not know exactly what these prophecies were. They could have been foretellings of the future, but that is an unlikely possibility. Generally, the prophecies were anything from preaching to simply talking together in group conversations. However they occurred, they were Spirit-led utterances of God's truth from one to another. We have no reason from the Bible to think that the Spirit has stopped leading us in this way, though we should have no desire for our meetings to look like those disorganized meetings in Corinth, which Paul was correcting here.

Paul wrote also that women should remain silent, at least in terms of the public evaluation of prophecies. Whatever the specifics of their silence, they were not to exercise authority in public. To do so would have been scandalous in Corinth, and Paul instructs against it elsewhere as well (see 1 Timothy 2), although it seems clear from chapter 11 that this silence was not absolute but simply a silence in positions of leadership. The women certainly should not have been yelling out questions to their husbands (14:35). Such questions, Paul wrote, whether directed to one's husband or to an elder or another teacher should be left for outside of the assembly.

In all of this, the church was to be ordered by Paul's teaching, recognizing it as from God (14:36–40). There is nothing inherently disorderly in desiring spiritual gifts, and there is nothing undesirable about expressing them in an orderly fashion. Passion and order can and should go together in our assembly in order to communicate the truth about God.

Love of order is not a passing intellectual fad, a relic of Western, enlightenment modernism. According to the Bible, it is part of the very nature of humanity because it is part of the nature of God himself. He himself is a God not of disorder but of peace. That is why we Christians desire things to be done in a decent, fitting, orderly way, because even in the way we do things, we communicate something of what God is like. God is holy; with him there is right and wrong. God is good; he is committed to punish what is wrong. God is our Creator; he made us. And he will judge us according to his unvarying goodness. At its best, human government reflects something of the order of God; and so do our families. We understand that life thrives where there is both authority and love. We Christians understand such order to be a reflection of God's own life within himself. We see in the Gospels the Son of God, Jesus Christ, submitting himself to the will of God the Father. Authority and love are joined together. Christians are to communicate something of this in sharing the gospel of Jesus Christ and to exemplify it in our individual lives, especially in our congregations.

My Christian brothers and sisters, do you see what this means for you? If you desire to give a message in tongues, seek out your pastor to talk about it. If you think that you have some intelligible message from the Lord, again, see your pastor or some other elder about it before acting on your understanding. Sisters, this is why we present men as leaders in this assembly—not to lord their authority over women but to present them as examples of humble, even countercultural, submission, which is submission to the authority of God's Word. We must be especially concerned that the women in our churches who have no husband will be able to come and talk to the elders to get the fellowship and guidance that they need. All of us should be reminded by this passage to study God's Word and to be shaped by it in how we fellowship and hold our meetings together. One guard against selfishness is the order that God has set in his church.

Unity

A second guard against selfishness in the church is a concern for unity. Paul writes:

> Now about spiritual gifts, brothers, I do not want you to be ignorant. You know that when you were pagans, somehow or other you were influenced and led astray to mute idols. Therefore I tell you that no one who is speaking by the Spirit of God says, 'Jesus be cursed.' And no one can say, 'Jesus is Lord,' except by the Holy Spirit. There are different kinds of gifts, but the same Spirit. There are different kinds of service, but the same Lord. There are different kinds of working, but the same God works all of them in all men. Now to each one the manifestation of the Spirit is given for the common good. To one there is given through the Spirit the message of wisdom, to another the message of knowledge by means of the same Spirit, to another faith by the same Spirit, to another gifts of healing by that one Spirit, to another miraculous powers, to another prophecy, to another distinguishing between spirits, to another speaking in different kinds of tongues, and to still another the interpretation of tongues. All these are the work of one and the same Spirit, and he gives them to each one, just as he determines. (1 Cor. 12:1–11)

In this passage we see that God values unity. We see also that we are to undermine selfish divisions in the church by realizing our unity. I recently read what I assume was a made-up anecdote about "a Welshman [who] was wrecked on a desert island. By the time he was rescued, he had built out of driftwood not only a house for himself, but a small town with a pub, a rugby club, and two small chapels. 'But why two chapels?' asked his rescuers. 'You see that one,' he replied. 'Well that's the one I don't go to.'"[2]

I don't know what you think of this issue of unity. Paul clearly knew how important it is for us. Our differing gifts might seem to divide us, but if they are exercised as God intends that will not be the case. We see here that we are united in God. We are united in allegiance to the same Lord, Jesus Christ (12:1–3, 5). We are united in recognizing the same Spirit as the gift-giver (12:4, 7a, 8–11), and we are united in recognizing the same God as the source of all (12:6). We are also united in our purpose—that of the common good (12:7; 14).

It seems that the Corinthians had also written to Paul about the "spirituals" (12:1), which refer to either spiritual gifts or to the self-styled spiritual people, those who were having and ostentatiously using some of these gifts. So Paul instructs the Corinthians about them. He does not want them to be divisive in their worship practices, like so much pagan worship was. Shards of pottery and clay and lead have been found with curses in the names of various Greek gods in Corinth, such as "Hermes curse Gaius." Perhaps Paul's words, "No one who is speaking by the Spirit of God says, 'Jesus be cursed,' and no one can say, 'Jesus is Lord,' except by the Holy Spirit" (12:3), were a reference to some young Christians trying to misuse Jesus to curse personal enemies. Whatever the meaning, Paul stresses here that the Christians are united by having the same Lord who is the same gift-giver and the same source of their new life.

The list of gifts we find here (12:8–10) is not meant to be a complete list of the *charismata*, the gifts of God's grace to us. There are many things in the New Testament called *charisma*, including God's gift of eternal life (Rom. 6:23) and even Paul's physical deliverance from shipwreck (2 Cor. 1:10–11). As Peter writes, "Each one should use whatever gift he has received to serve others, faithfully administering God's grace in its various forms" (1 Pet. 4:10). Space does not allow us to go over each gift listed here, and I am not sure that Paul means absolutely distinct things by each one. "Prophecy" seems to have a wide range of meanings in the New Testament. Here in this epistle we might interpret "prophecy" as basically the Spirit-inspired teaching of God's Word to others, including both longer, prepared statements and shorter, extemporaneous comments.

As for the Corinthian practice of speaking in tongues, we do not see it talked about in other letters. There are occasions in Acts of people speaking in tongues upon their initial conversion, but those tongues were ones that others could understand. Additionally, those occurrences seem to have been part of God's plan to do something dramatic to demonstrate the entry of people into his kingdom and thereby into the church. First Corinthians is the only place in the New Testament where we get the idea that such ecstatic tongues might be a part of a weekly public service.

Should we be encouraging people to speak in tongues today (12:10; 14:5, 18)? I don't think so. In 1 Corinthians Paul often takes the "yes, but . . ." way of making his argument. He concedes a point but then restates it to get them on course. He did that in his discussion about judging teachers and one another generally; he also did it in his discussions about freedom to eat meat offered to idols and freedom to marry or abstain from marriage. He will do it again in chapter 16, when he covers the practice of "baptism for the dead." Paul, under the inspiration of the Holy Spirit, understands this gift of tongues to be something from God, but Paul's point here is that Christians should pray that God's Spirit will work among us in whatever way he might desire. And normally, according to what Paul teaches in this letter, such work will be geared toward the edification of the church as a whole. "All these are the work of one and the same Spirit, and he gives them to each one, just as he determines" (12:11; cf. 4:7).

Jesus Christ lived a perfect life and died on the cross bearing God's correct wrath against sinners, and Christ did that for every sinner who will ever turn away from sins and trust him in his sacrifice. That is what he calls us to do. His own Spirit, the Spirit we read of in these verses, gives us new life in connection with hearing this news. We repent of our sins and trust Christ and so are saved from the punishment due us. We are restored in our relationship with God, and we are filled with God's own Spirit. Just to be clear here, we Christians understand ourselves to be united together by actually sharing in the same Spirit, God's Spirit indwelling us. This is how we are meant to live. Blood is thicker than water, we say. Well, also, the Spirit is thicker than blood!

Loneliness is a crushing reality for many people. But, my friend, I want to tell you that the loneliness you experience—at work, in your sins, even in the carnal embrace of a prostitute—is meant to cause you dissatisfaction. That loneliness is meant to turn you to God so that you can be filled by his

Spirit and enfolded in the fellowship of his saints. There is more nearness in the conversation of two sisters in Christ after a morning worship service, sharing, as they do, God's Spirit, than anyone can know in even the most intimate carnal relationship.

We do well to meditate on the unity we have in Christ. Consider what makes you feel divided from fellow church members. How would meditating on the realities Paul lays out here help you? Let us beware in our congregations of those natural, carnal fault lines between us and work to overcome them. Practice thanking God for the diversity of gifts evidenced in your church. We can undermine selfish divisions in the church by considering our unity in God.

Mutuality

A third guard against selfishness in the church is a focus on mutuality, which is what Paul talks about in verses 12–30. When he nears the end of the passage, he asks a series of questions: "Are all apostles? Are all prophets? Are all teachers? Do all work miracles? Do all have gifts of healing? Do all speak in tongues? Do all interpret?" (vv. 29–30). The answer to all these questions is an implied no. What we find here is a focus on mutuality. Paul calls Christians to undermine selfish envy by realizing their mutual dependence on each other.

Of course, the envy that Paul warns of in the passage ignores the importance of our own role. Paul introduces the image of the church as the body of Christ, an image he was introduced to by the risen Christ when Jesus asked Paul, "Why do you persecute me?" (Acts 9:4). So here Paul tells the Corinthians that we are all part of one body with one Spirit (1 Cor. 12:4–6), an image he then stretches out over several verses. The body is made up of many parts; an envious dissatisfaction with the part we are does not make us any less a part of the body. We need to trust God in the way he has arranged the parts. Think of how the church would be harmed if we all had only the gift you are now envying! Your role may be more important than you have considered. Of course, there is always the opposite problem of pride, which ignores the importance of the role of others: "The eye cannot say to the hand, 'I don't need you!' And the head cannot say to the feet, 'I don't need you!'" (v. 21).

Paul says that our envy should be replaced by a godly sympathy, a sort of "one for all and all for one" in the church:

God has combined the members of the body and has given greater honor to the parts that lacked it, so that there should be no division in the body, but that its parts should have equal concern for each other. If one part suffers, every part suffers with it; if one part is honored, every part rejoices with it. Now you are the body of Christ, and each one of you is a part of it. (vv. 24–27)

The church should not be marked by division but by concern for each member. This is a key principle that Paul has been teaching the Corinthians throughout this letter (cf. 1:10; 3:3; 11:18). That is why, as he writes in 12:26, suffering and joy are shared by all.

We must in our congregations covenant to live with each other in this way. The inside front cover of the hymnals in my church contains a line that reads, "We will rejoice at each other's happiness, and endeavor with tenderness and sympathy to bear each other's burdens and sorrows." Similarly, all of Paul's instructions in this epistle presuppose a context of committed relationships, a context that was alien to the pagan religions already in Corinth when the gospel came. Except for the occasion of great public feasts, one worshiped pagan gods simply by making sacrificial offerings on a whim. How different the Christian congregation is! It is a body. It assembles together regularly. Christians are part of the one body, and we must give testimony to this truth in the weekly rhythm of our lives as we congregate. Envy must be replaced by godly sympathy.

Envy also usurps God's role; he is the one who has appointed the variance in gifts: "In the church God has appointed first of all apostles, second prophets, third teachers, then workers of miracles, also those having gifts of healing, those able to help others, those with gifts of administration, and those speaking in different kinds of tongues" (v. 28). Clearly the order of gifts here is significant, especially the first three—apostles, prophets, and teachers.

The rest of the list consists of various others gifts God gives his church. Paul clearly understood that the role of apostle would not continue indefinitely in each congregation. If he had thought otherwise, it is likely he would have used "apostleship" rather than "prophecy" when he wrote, "Follow the way of love and eagerly desire spiritual gifts, especially the gift of prophecy" (14:1). In the New Testament the word *apostle* is used of a limited group, those who were witnesses to the resurrection and their messengers. The New Testament nowhere teaches that there are individuals outside of a particular congregation whom all congregations are to obey, except for the apostles themselves in their instructions, and even then they appeal to the congregation as a unified group to confirm their witness, as Paul did when writing to the Galatians (see Galatians 1). Each church member has various gifts, and to envy someone else's gift is to usurp God's role in giving these gifts, as if we knew better than God.

This all may sound a little bit like the modern desire in our culture for diversity, but Paul does not laud diversity for diversity's sake; rather, the differences in gifting among church members is a divinely ordered diversity, one with a purpose—that of revealing the nature of God himself.

My Christian friends, beware of ingratitude about how God has gifted you. Instead, rejoice with others. How have you helped someone else bear their sorrow this month? Fight envy. Covenant together with others in your church to fight selfishness and to build a congregational shape to your discipleship. Let us undermine selfish envy by considering our God-designed, mutual dependence on each other.

Love

A fourth guard against selfishness in the church is love. We undermine selfish pride by loving others. He is about to overarch everything he has just said about spiritual gifting with the importance of love, what he calls "the most excellent way" (12:31). He begins:

> If I speak in the tongues of men and of angels, but have not love, I am only a resounding gong or a clanging cymbal. If I have the gift of prophecy and can fathom all mysteries and all knowledge, and if I have a faith that can move mountains, but have not love, I am nothing. If I give all I possess to the poor and surrender my body to the flames, but have not love, I gain nothing. (13:1–3)

Love is necessary, he says here. Loveless tongues are nothing (13:1); loveless prophecy is nothing (13:2a); loveless faith is nothing (13:2b); even loveless social action or martyrdom are nothing (13:3). He continues his description in terms both positive and negative. Love is patient and kind; love is not envious, boastful, proud, rude, self-seeking, easily angered, or grudge-bearing. Love does not delight in evil but rejoices with the truth. It always protects, trusts, hopes, and perseveres. (vv. 4–7).

Finally, Paul says, love lasts (vv. 8–13). Love outlasts prophecy, tongues, and knowledge. Our imperfect prophecy and knowledge will be put away. They are only partial, after all, and will eventually be fulfilled and perfected—not,

I think, as some have suggested, at the completion of the canon of Scripture, but at the passing of the saint into the presence of God, or at the second coming of Christ when maturity will replace childishness (v. 11). But although prophecy and knowledge will pass away, love will remain, even in the rarified celestial atmosphere of the unmediated presence of God. When sight and knowledge are perfected, when our senses are filled full, then we will see how love is even greater than faith and hope. Then we will know and taste and experience love. Love is what we know in our relationship with God when we see him most perfectly.

Jonathan Edwards preached a series of sermons on 1 Corinthians 13. In fact, it was during that series that his town of Northampton, Massachusetts, knew great awakening and revival spiritually. He entitled his final sermon in the series, "Heaven Is a World of Love." It is a world of love, because God the fountain of love dwells there most especially:

> There in heaven, this infinite fountain of love—this eternal Three in One—is set open without any obstacle to hinder access to it, as it flows for ever. . . . And there this glorious fountain for ever flows forth in streams, yea, in rivers of love and delight, and these rivers swell, as it were, to an ocean of love, in which the souls of the ransomed may bathe with the sweetest enjoyment, and their hearts, as it were, be deluged with love![3]

In heaven, Edwards reflected, there will be only lovely objects, and those will be perfectly lovely. There, he says, "shall be all those objects that the saints have set their hearts upon, and which they have loved above all things while in this world."[4] "In every heart in heaven, love dwells and reigns."[5] Heaven is a world of holy, divine, and perfect love. In heaven the love is always mutual, never interrupted nor dampened by jealousy. There shall be nothing to clog or hinder the saints in the exercises and expressions of love. Love will there be expressed in perfect decency and wisdom. Love will be perfectly enjoyed there, forever uninterrupted. "In heaven, all things shall conspire to promote their love."[6] The fruit of this love will be perfect behavior toward God and one another, perfect tranquility and joy. My friend, ultimate love requires the ultimate object of our love. We are made for God, and it is Christ who shows us how to love.

My Christian brother or sister, do these characteristics of love describe you? I imagine many of you are familiar with the exercise of substituting your name for the word "love" in Paul's description to see if the description is true of you: "Mary is patient . . . Liam is kind . . . Helen does not envy

. . . Kyle does not boast . . . Emily is not proud . . . Jovan is not rude . . . Jennifer is not self-seeking . . . Rashieda is not easily angered . . . Julie-Anne keeps no record of wrongs . . . Stephen does not delight in evil . . . Dixie rejoices with the truth . . . Nathaniel always protects . . . Wayne always trusts . . . Bernadette always hopes . . . Jean-Marie always perseveres."

First Corinthians 13 is a great resource to use for mediation. The list of love characteristics Paul gives can also lead us to confession. It is a marvelous tool for thanksgiving and for making intercession for ourselves and others. It is also a great list to use in guiding our praises of God, for who better than the Lord Jesus Christ has personified this love?

> Thou Who wast rich beyond all splendour,
> All for love's sake becamest poor;
> Thrones for a manger didst surrender,
> Sapphire-paved courts for stable floor.
> Thou Who wast rich beyond all splendour;
> All for love's sake becamest poor.

How are we reflecting this love in our churches? Jesus said that this is how the world would know that we are his disciples, by the love we have for one another (John 13:34–35). This kind of love is vital to our evangelistic task. It is essential to our displaying God's character and to bringing him glory. Without this love we are nothing. Love undermines selfishness.

Edification

The fifth guard against selfishness in the church is edification (14:1–26). In chapter 14 Paul exhorts the Corinthians to battle against selfishness by focusing on edification. We undermine a selfish focus by edifying the church. Edifying the church is loving the church, Paul says, so we should pray for hearts that are set on edifying one another.

According to Paul, edifying the church happens through prophecy rather than through uninterpreted tongues:

For anyone who speaks in a tongue does not speak to men but to God. Indeed, no one understands him; he utters mysteries with his spirit. But everyone who prophesies speaks to men for their strengthening, encouragement and comfort. He who speaks in a tongue edifies himself, but he who prophesies edifies the church. I would like every one of you to speak in tongues, but I would rather have you prophesy. He who prophesies is greater than one who speaks in tongues, unless he interprets, so that the church may be edified. Now, brothers, if I come to you and speak in tongues, what good will I be to you, unless I bring you some revelation or knowledge or prophecy or word of instruction? (vv. 2–6)

The church is built up by Spirit-led utterances of truth in languages we can understand. Such utterances build up the body more than speaking in unknown tongues. Paul is not commending a private prayer language; he is writing about what builds up the church. Edifying the church requires understanding (14:7–11), which is why Paul writes, "Unless you speak intelligible words with your tongue, how will anyone know what you are saying? You will just be speaking into the air" (v. 9). When you seek and pray for certain gifts, edifying the church should be your goal: "Try to excel in gifts that build up the church" (v. 12). Edifying the church is the point of gathering together as a body (vv. 13–20). Tongues without interpretation edify no one but the one speaking. Think about this carefully, he urges them.

Even unbelievers are better served by intelligible speech than by words that are unintelligible, which is the point of Paul's next words (vv. 21–25). Unknown tongues serve as signs of God's judgment on unbelievers, just as the unknown tongues of the foreign invaders served as signs of God's judgment on the unbelieving Israelites in the prophecy of Isaiah. Furthermore, Paul recognizes that unbelievers will think Christians are crazy if they come to a church where everyone is speaking in tongues. Verse 23 is as simple as that. Prophecy, on the other hand, as it extols God and shares the gospel of Christ, is used to convict and convert.

Finally, Paul says that edifying the church is everybody's work: "What then shall we say, brothers? When you come together, everyone has a hymn, or a word of instruction, a revelation, a tongue or an interpretation. All of these must be done for the strengthening of the church" (v. 26). Everything that occurs in our meetings should be done for the purpose of strengthening the church. Brothers and sisters, do you go to church each Sunday with the purpose of edifying the church, to build up those around you? Be eager to exercise your gifts in ways that build up the church. It is fine to participate in one of those spiritual gifts inventories that bring out what you like to do and what you think you are good at. But consider also what others think you are good at, and consider what is needed in the church. Study God's Word and pray that God will use you to encourage others by it.

The principle of edification must also underlie our choice of church elders. We must look for men who are clearly living for the good of others and who serve others by knowing and teaching Scripture. But even with solid elders in place, every believer is called to participate in building up their particular congregation. We gather on Sunday mornings to praise God and to encourage each other, which is not selfish. It glorifies God and gives strength and comfort to everyone there.

Fight selfishness in the church by giving yourself to biblical order, to unity, to mutuality, to love, and to edification. Let us pray that our congregations will be good heralds and living displays of this good news.

11

DEATH

1 CORINTHIANS 15

My friend C. J. Mahaney concluded a three-part sermon series on the afterlife on a Sunday that happened to coincide with Mother's Day. C. J. had not connected the holiday with his prospective topic or with his sermon title, which was simply "Hell." Needless to say, some mothers were not encouraged in the way they had expected to be upon coming to church that Sunday. This little story is meant to serve as a lead-in to the theme of this chapter—death.

Thus far in our study of the church and her challenges, we have focused on those posed by division, imposters, and sin. All of those challenges in various forms were confronting the church in Corinth at the time of Paul's epistle. But there was another challenge that we come to now, which is the Corinthians' perspective on death. The Corinthians believed in death more than they believed in the resurrection. Some had, in fact, even gone so far as to deny the resurrection of the dead, which, Paul knew, was to deny something at the very heart of the Christian faith.

The reality of death was not in dispute, nor were its pain and ugliness. In dispute was whether there is anything after death. Many people today say no. In one recent Japanese poll 82 percent answered no when asked if they believe in life after death. Of course, Christianity as a religion is all tied up with death, and yet Christianity is not just about death; it is also about resurrection. This life is full of death, and the passing nature of everything in the world is painful for us. But while death is the frustration of this life, the hope of the resurrection is an undiluted good.

As we come to the end of our study in 1 Corinthians, we find ourselves now in the last portion of the main theological teaching of the epistle, which also happens to be the most extended treatment in the Bible on the resurrection. And as we examine 1 Corinthians 15, we want to notice three things: (1) the resurrection is an essential part of the Christian message; (2) the resurrection is an essential part of the Christian life; and (3) the resurrection is real.

The Resurrection and the Gospel

The first assertion Paul makes in this famous chapter is that the resurrection is an essential part of the good news. Paul's topic in the first eleven verses of chapter 15 is the gospel that Paul preached and the Corinthians believed. He begins by clarifying that the Corinthians' continued adherence to this message is essential to their salvation: "Now, brothers, I want to remind you of the gospel I preached to you, which you received and on which you have taken your stand. By this gospel you are saved, if you hold firmly to the word I preached to you. Otherwise, you have believed in vain" (vv. 1–2). Here, at the beginning of the chapter, Paul challenges them to hold firm. We will see at the end of the chapter that he tells them to stand firm.

Paul continues, describing the word that must be firmly held: "What I received I passed on to you as of first importance: that Christ died for our sins according to the Scriptures, that he was buried, that he was raised on the third day according to the Scriptures" (v. 3). This is the nub of the gospel, the basic message of Christianity. The Scriptures that Paul references comprise the Old Testament, which predicted Christ's crucifixion and resurrection.

First Corinthians is a letter written to a Christian church on subjects that are of interest to very few. The death of Christ, as absorbing a topic as that might be to Christians, is simply a historical fact to others. Christ himself, though tremendously significant in history, simply does not attract much interest outside of superficial acknowledgment at that time of year when we sing about Bethlehem and sheep. But one word in verse 3, "sins," bears eternal weight for everyone. All people are made in God's image, and we all have the capacity to know him. Perhaps we all have something of an innate desire to know God. But all of us have sinned, and that sin, which is disobedience to God, separates us from him and leaves us open to judgment.

But that is where Christ comes in. He was born in Bethlehem and grew up to live a perfect life, and then he died on the cross to bear God's judgment, wrath, and punishment as a substitute for all of those who would ever turn from their sins and trust in him. By his resurrection from the dead, we know that he exhausted God's claims against all those who turn and trust in him—in Christ, our incarnated and crucified and risen Lord, who saves us from our sins' deserved punishment. My Christian friend, note the objective, historical content of the gospel. The Christian message is not just another worldview. It is not fundamentally about how you find success in your job, fulfillment in your marriage, or a cure from your insomnia. It is about something Christ did for us—he died for our sins.

The reason we know this is that Christ was raised (v. 4). Paul writes of the eyewitnesses that confirmed Christ's resurrection:

> He appeared to Peter, and then to the Twelve. After that, he appeared to more than five hundred of the brothers at the same time, most of whom are still living, though some have fallen asleep. Then he appeared to James, then to all the apostles, and last of all he appeared to me also, as to one abnormally born. (vv. 5–8)

Paul adds, "For I am the least of the apostles and do not even deserve to be called an apostle, because I persecuted the church of God. But by the grace of God I am what I am, and his grace to me was not without effect. No, I worked harder than all of them—yet not I, but the grace of God that was with me" (vv. 9–10). Here was Paul, the former persecutor of Christians, now preaching with zeal and giving his whole life to it. How could this be possible? Only by God's strength working in him. Paul finishes this section of the letter by repeating the reminder that he had given the Corinthians in verse 1—this is a message that they had believed.

Many scholars refer to these opening verses of chapter 15 as the earliest Christian creed, especially verses 3 to 5. The verses are structured as five parallel phrases affirming Christ's death, burial, resurrection, and witnesses to that resurrection. Paul probably wrote this letter around A.D. 51. He had preached to them some months earlier, or even a year or two earlier, and even then the message was already established. It is clear then that the basic

Christian gospel was not developed in the first few centuries after Christ, as some people have suggested. Rather, it is the message that revolutionized the Mediterranean world in the first century.

This is the great message through which God has revolutionized our lives. It is what we have believed. We know this message. Note the importance of the objective historical content of the gospel: Jesus Christ himself claimed to be God incarnate. New Testament scholar Don Carson says that Jesus basically told his disciples, "When you look at the sketch of God from the Old Testament, you will see a likeness of me." God himself came in Christ. He is Emmanuel, God with us. Christianity is all tied up with these historical particulars—a real person who made a real claim, who died and was raised. Oh, my brothers and sisters, make it your goal to know this gospel and to share it with others, even as Paul did with these Corinthians.

Many congregations cite the Apostles' Creed or the Nicene Creed as part of their worship service, and by so doing, they are affirming their acceptance of the Christian gospel, the good news about Jesus Christ. And we affirm what we read here in Paul's epistle, that the resurrection of Jesus Christ is an essential part of that good news.

The Resurrection and the Christian Life

As Paul continues defending the importance of the resurrection, he makes clear that not only is it an essential part of the Christian message, but it is also an essential part of the Christian life (vv. 12–34). Some of the Corinthians were saying that there was no resurrection from the dead. Although the resurrection is the last theological topic in this amazing letter, Paul might have seen it as the root of so many of the other matters he has already addressed. Perhaps that is why he lays out the many problems that would immediately arise for the Christian if in fact there were no resurrection. If Christ has not been raised from the dead, the consequences are terrible.

First, if Christ has not been raised from the dead, then, Paul writes, all his preaching has been for nothing: "But if it is preached that Christ has been raised from the dead, how can some of you say that there is no resurrection of the dead? If there is no resurrection of the dead, then not even Christ has been raised. And if Christ has not been raised, our preaching is useless and so is your faith" (vv. 12–14). With no resurrection, Paul's preaching is in vain. Furthermore, he says, without the resurrection, the faith of the Corinthians is all in vain. "If Christ has not been raised, our preaching is useless *and so is your faith.*"

But it's not just Paul and the Corinthians who would be affected if Christ had in fact not been raised from the dead. Without the resurrection the apostles would be liars:

> More than that, we are then found to be false witnesses about God, for we have testified about God that he raised Christ from the dead. But he did not raise him if in fact the dead are not raised. For if the dead are not raised, then Christ has not been raised either. (vv. 15–16)

If there is no resurrection, Paul and all the apostles and others who claimed to have witnessed the resurrected Christ are liars.

But there is more. If the resurrection did not happen, then the Corinthians' hopes for forgiveness are in vain. "And if Christ has not been raised, your faith is futile; you are still in your sins" (v. 17). Paul writes elsewhere that Christ was "delivered over to death for our sins and was raised to life for our justification" (Rom. 4:25). He died as a substitute, paying our debt, and he was raised confirming our justification. Christ's resurrection completes his work of securing God's blessing for his people. If there was no resurrection, there is no assurance of any divine blessing of forgiveness. My friends, what things do you hope to obtain this year? The iPod may be nice; the computer you may need; the kitchen gadget you may like; the camera you may use; but there is nothing you need more than the gift of forgiveness for your sins. Furthermore, if there is no resurrection of the dead, believers who have already died are lost: "Then those also who have fallen asleep in Christ are lost" (v. 18).

Paul also points out that apart from the resurrection, some of the Corinthians' practices are contradictory: "Now if there is no resurrection, what will those do who are baptized for the dead? If the dead are not raised at all, why are people baptized for them?" (v. 29). Baptizing for the dead is a worthless practice if the dead are not raised. We are not sure exactly what Paul was referring to here. We have no other evidence from the New Testament or from the early church of people who were baptized in proxy for someone else, living or dead. Paul may be saying, "Why follow this faith that contains the resurrection if now you are denying the resurrection?" His meaning could even be as simple as this: "Why baptize someone who is going to perish for eternity? What's the point?" This is how early church preachers like Tertullian and Chrysostom took Paul's words here. Whatever he meant exactly, Paul's point is that the very practices of the Corinthians themselves were inconsistent with the denial of a resurrection.

Without the resurrection, Paul's entire life would be pointless. Self-denial such as Paul demonstrated throughout his ministry—his giving of himself and his life's energy so fully for this one thing—is inconsistent with there being no resurrection. He writes:

> And as for us, why do we endanger ourselves every hour? I die every day—I mean that, brothers—just as surely as I glory [boast] over you in Christ Jesus our Lord. If I fought wild beasts in Ephesus for merely human reasons, what have I gained? If the dead are not raised, "Let us eat and drink, for tomorrow we die." (vv. 30–32)

Paul's boast here sounds a bit like what the psalmist said to God: "Yet for your sake we face death all day long; we are considered as sheep to be slaughtered" (Ps. 44:22). In fact, Paul used that verse when he wrote to the Romans a few years later. Here in Corinthians Paul writes, "I die every day," indicating his constant self-denial for the advancement of the gospel. He demonstrated self-denial in Corinth as he had in Ephesus where he had faced a riot, which might be what he is referring to in his statement about having fought wild beasts in Ephesus. All of this is pointless if the dead are not raised.

He summarizes succinctly by saying that Christians are the most pitiable people in the world if there is no resurrection: "If only for this life we have hope in Christ, we are to be pitied more than all men" (v. 19).

People ponder Pascal's Wager—Blaise Pascal's theory that it is a better bet to believe that God exists than not to believe, because the expected value of believing is always greater than the expected value of not believing—and they see Christianity as such a good, moral system of absolutes, one that provides meaning, peace of mind, and social benefits. Such people would be glad to be Christians, so long as all that stands behind it isn't true. Such people see Christianity as a useful delusion. But Paul could not disagree more. If the resurrection is not true, we have spent our lives for a lie. We have made a foolish investment. Paul knew of Christ's penetrating question, "What good will it be for a man if he gains the whole world, yet forfeits his soul?" (Matt. 16:26), and he was leaning his whole life into the truth of the gospel of the crucifixion and resurrection of Jesus Christ for our salvation.

My Christian friend, there is no doubt that death is one of the greatest challenges we face. Death feels unnatural and wrong, and according to the

Christian gospel, death is wrong. The resurrection is our great hope—a new life forever with God. As someone recently wrote:

> If the Bible is merely a collection of human thoughts, imaginings, and desires, the atheists are right—it is a contemptible piece of literature, perhaps the most contemptible ever constructed. It has inspired untold millions of people to put themselves and others through immense suffering, and sometimes death, in pursuit of a ludicrous and indeed nonexistent salvation.[1]

Brothers and sisters, the good news is that this salvation does exist, and it is wonderful. Suffering will give way to glory, and our frustrations and pains here will give way to fulfillment and satisfaction and joy forevermore in the presence of God. Stoke your love for God and desires for his presence and give time to cultivating that self-denying love that actively chips away and exports your heart from the concerns of this world to eternal concerns.

Right in the middle of this passage, Paul inserts the truth that the resurrection has taken place, and he traces out the trajectory of history from this stunning fact. Over against the resurrection deniers in the Corinthian church, Paul says forcefully:

> But Christ has indeed been raised from the dead, the firstfruits of those who have fallen asleep. For since death came through a man, the resurrection of the dead comes also through a man. For as in Adam all die, so in Christ all will be made alive. But each in his own turn: Christ, the firstfruits; then, when he comes, those who belong to him. Then the end will come, when he hands over the kingdom to God the Father after he has destroyed all dominion, authority and power. For he must reign until he has put all his enemies under his feet. The last enemy to be destroyed is death. For he "has put everything under his feet." Now when it says that "everything" has been put under him, it is clear that this does not include God himself, who put everything under Christ. When he has done this, then the Son himself will be made subject to him who put everything under him, so that God may be all in all. (vv. 20–28)

Paul gets this image of firstfruits from the Old Testament. The firstfruits were the first portion of the grain the Israelites harvested, the portion they would take and give to the priest (see Lev. 23:10). Christ's resurrection is the down payment, the preview, the first installment, the beginning of the general resurrection. Paul points out that we all died in Adam, and now in Christ we are all made alive, that is, all of those who belong to Christ, all who have repented of their sins and trusted in Christ.

What a splendid, majestic, glorious picture is painted here before our eyes. Here we have the promise that Christ will destroy and annihilate all opposition to God—both in people and in fallen structures. God's authority has been committed to the Son to do this conquering. Christ is the one who from his throne rules all the world alone. This rule has been committed to him so that he will then turn the kingdom over to God the Father. Paul seems to have in his mind here a verse so frequently quoted by Jesus: "The LORD said to my Lord, 'Sit at my right hand until I make your enemies a footstool for your feet'" (Ps. 110:1). Christ's reign continues on from the resurrection, continues, as one hymn says, "conquering and to conquer," until it culminates in the reign of God through all creation. The purpose of Christ's coming was to teach and model, to live and die, to rise and reign. Though Christ reigns now, that reign is partially hidden; it is not yet complete in all its purposes. But the day is coming when it will be, and more than anything else it is his resurrection that points us toward this great hope. So Paul, along with the psalmist (Ps. 8:6), says of Christ, the perfect man, "You made him ruler over the works of your hands; you put everything under his feet" (v. 27).

Do you see the big picture here? Death came through a man, life comes through a man, and the end of history is the exaltation of God. What do you think of the vastness of this understanding of history? Is there something attractive to you in its grandeur? If so, it might be wishful thinking, or it could be that you were made for much more than just this world. You were made to love and serve the victorious Son of God who ultimately, as we read here, subjects himself to the Father.

When Paul writes that Christ, the Son of God, submits, or subjects, himself to God, he uses the same word that the Bible uses for the subjection of children to parents, wives to husbands, and church members to elders. There is no denigration in this sort of subjection, either for people or for Christ. There is no devaluing, nothing shameful or wrong or degrading or insulting. God's glory is displayed, as we saw earlier, in the structure of order. While certainly in this fallen world order can be wrong and harmful, order itself can be a wonderful reflection of God, and even of God himself within the Trinity.

Brothers and sisters, consider the wonderful future we have and the great fuel that such confidence in that future is in our lives. Are you sustained by this hope? Do you find yourself encouraged to continue even amidst stumbles? Do you put yourself around friends who will encourage you in this great hope? Paul writes, "Do not be misled: 'Bad company corrupts good character.' Come back to your senses as you ought, and stop sinning; for there are some who are ignorant of God—I say this to your shame" (vv. 33–34). Paul cites here a popular line from an Athenian play by Menander.[2] Brothers and sisters, find friends who encourage you in this hope, and make them your best friends.

True Christian congregations are built on the reality of the resurrection of Jesus Christ and the reality of our own coming resurrection through him. The reality of the resurrection is why, when a church member dies, we do not grieve as those who have no hope (1 Thess. 4:13). It is why we preach as we do. If the body of Jesus of Nazareth lies decomposed in some ancient burial site in the Middle East, we are all wasting our time, but the fact that it does not should change our lives.

Friends, it is the hope we have in the risen and reigning Christ that must shape our congregations. Because we understand that all of history and all of reality is centered on God—culminating in him, his glory, his pleasure—God's children are taken up into that same love that God experiences forever in himself—Father loving Son and Son loving Father, Father loving the Spirit and the Spirit loving the Father, and Son loving the Spirit and the Spirit loving the Son. This is the perfect love that is the Christian's destiny. The resurrection of Jesus Christ is what cracks open the door of our dark world from the place of overflowing light and truth and love and hope and goodness and beauty in the future, which we are called into through Christ.

That is why the Christian church gathers on Sundays. The most fundamental Christian calendar is not annual; it is weekly, because Christ rose on the first day of the week. In celebration of that we gather on the first morning of each week to rejoice together in that great hope of the resurrection of and through Jesus Christ. The resurrection makes a big difference not just in our theology but in how we live our lives.

The Resurrection Is Real

That the resurrection of the body will be a reality for believers is the truth Paul uses to complete his teaching in this section of the epistle. The resurrection is a bodily resurrection. Immortality was a common idea in the ancient world of Athens and Corinth and Ephesus and Rome, but not all religions and philosophies taught it. Epicureanism, for example, taught annihilation at death; people just cease to exist. A common epitaph on ancient tombs from this era is this simple inscription: "I was not, I was, I am not, I care not." Even for those who believed in immortality, it was an immortality with no body. The idea of a bodily resurrection was unexpected, unattractive, curious, disgusting to the point of revolting, and just plain weird to the ancient Greeks. It was very nearly unthinkable, as we find out in the book of Acts:

> Some of them asked, "What is this babbler trying to say?" Others remarked, "He seems to be advocating foreign gods." They said this because Paul was preaching the good news about Jesus and the resurrection. Then they took him and brought him to a meeting of the Areopagus, where they said to him, "May we know what this new teaching is that you are presenting? You are bringing some strange ideas to our ears, and we want to know what they mean." (Acts 17:18–20)

Other translations say that those who heard Paul in Athens "sneered," "mocked," or "scoffed" at the idea of a bodily resurrection. In fact, among the ancient Near Eastern religions that found a home on the streets of Corinth, only Judaism taught a bodily resurrection.

The resurrection of the body is not mentioned much in the Old Testament, but where it is, it represents important things about God himself, such as his sovereign victory, in Isaiah 26, and the vindication of his righteous character, in Daniel 12.

Paul continues his discussion to the Corinthians, answering the argument of those who denied the possibility of resurrection by the fact that dead bodies decay. Paul provides this counterargument from nature:

> But someone may ask, "How are the dead raised? With what kind of body will they come?" How foolish! What you sow does not come to life unless it dies. When you sow, you do not plant the body that will be, but just a seed, perhaps of wheat or of something else. But God gives it a body as he has determined, and to each kind of seed he gives its own body. (vv. 35–38)

And then Paul goes on to describe the resurrection body:

> All flesh is not the same: Men have one kind of flesh, animals have another, birds another and fish another. There are also heavenly bodies and there are earthly bodies; but the splendor of the heavenly bodies is one kind, and the splendor of the earthly bodies is another. The sun has one kind of splendor, the moon another and the stars another; and star differs from star in splendor. So will it be with the resurrection of the dead. (vv. 39–42a)

Paul first counters the anti-resurrection arguments using analogies, and then he elaborates on some of the differences between the earthly body and the resurrection body: "The body that is sown is perishable, it is raised imperishable; it is sown in dishonor, it is raised in glory; it is sown in weakness, it is raised in power; it is sown a natural body, it is raised a spiritual body. If there is a natural body, there is also a spiritual body" (v. 42b).

In sum, Paul explains that in the resurrection we will have a body but not a physical body. It will be spiritual, powerful, glorious, imperishable—a body very different from the one we have in this life. The best way for Paul to solidify his argument was by pointing to an example of a resurrected body—the risen Christ. So Paul sets out an analogy using Adam and Christ:

> So it is written: "The first man Adam became a living being"; the last Adam, a life-giving spirit. The spiritual did not come first, but the natural, and after that the spiritual. The first man was of the dust of the earth, the second man from heaven. As was the earthly man, so are those who are of the earth; and as is the man from heaven, so also are those who are of heaven. And just as we have borne the likeness of the earthly man, so shall we bear the likeness of the man from heaven. (vv. 45–49)

Paul takes the account in Genesis 2:7 of man's creation from the dust of the earth, and he contrasts it with the man who came not from dust but from heaven (cf. Dan. 7:13).

It is this second one, the man from heaven, that we will be like, Paul explains (vv. 50–57).

Paul presents to us that last great day that will come with the victorious sounding of a trumpet: "Listen, I tell you a mystery: We will not all sleep, but we will all be changed—in a flash, in the twinkling of an eye, at the last trumpet. For the trumpet will sound, the dead will be raised imperishable, and we will be changed" (vv. 51–52; cf. Isa. 27:13; Joel 2:1; Zeph. 1:14–16). Our new bodies will be imperishable and immortal, death having been swallowed up forever and with it all tears and disgrace (Isa. 25:8).

Paul quotes the Lord's exulting over death from Hosea 13:14: "Where, O death, is your victory? Where, O death, is your sting?" The Lord Jesus Christ has brought us victory over the correct charges of the law against us by bearing our sins and being raised to make us right with God. John Donne's poem gives us a taste of this exultation:

> Death, be not proud, though some have called thee
> Mighty and dreadful, for, thou art not so; . . .

One short sleep past, we wake eternally,
And death shall be no more; death, thou shalt die.

I wonder why unbelievers will not accept this testimony about the resurrection. It was this very thing that many years ago led me to embrace Christianity. A good book on the subject is *The Case for Christ: A Journalist's Personal Investigation of the Evidence for Jesus* by Lee Strobel.[3] Friend, you were never made to find full satisfaction in this life. You were made for God. And you can find your way back to him, or better, he will find you, through Jesus Christ, the last Adam, the man from heaven. The manger is not the end of the story; the manger led to a grave and through it to the resurrection.

What blessings we have pictured here for us—an imperishable, glorious, powerful, spiritual body. We will be changed, a certain, guaranteed change, from mortal to immortal, from sinful to victorious over all sin and death through Christ. My Christian brothers and sisters, this is the greatest gift you will ever receive. As Christians, our best days are most assuredly ahead of us. There will come a day when everything that causes disgrace or tears will be taken away. Do you see the confidence that we can have as believers because we will end up around the throne rejoicing? No problem that you have is unsolvable to God.

The work of his Spirit, which he has already begun in you here, he will complete in you there, making you perfectly loving as you perfectly know his love, perfectly peaceful as you perfectly know his peace, and perfectly joyful as you perfectly know his joy. That, my Christian brothers and sisters, is our most certain fate in Christ. We as a church are a community of people who believe in Christ, and we see death as a challenge, not a defeat. Understanding death changes our outlook on life. We believe in a real resurrection.

Conclusion: Stand Firm

"Therefore, my dear brothers, stand firm. Let nothing move you. Always give yourselves fully to the work of the Lord, because you know that your labor in the Lord is not in vain" (v. 58). Paul knew that their standing firm in the doctrine concerning the resurrection would result in necessary changes in their lives. Have you learned that? Doctrine and life go together in the work of the Lord. If you want to stand firm, you need to hold firm, especially to the great truth of the resurrection.

Harriet Tubman, a type of Moses to African-American slaves, once described for a reporter a funeral she had attended. She recounted a stirring section of the sermon preached there, which told about how death will never eventually find everybody. Tubman said that the sermon led to a dance, a "spiritual shuffle," in which every member of the congregation shook hands with every other member, using personal names in song:

> My sis'r Mary's boun' to go.
> My sis'r Nanny's boun' to go.
> My brudder Tony's boun' to go.
> My brudder Julie's boun' to go.[4]

Death would mock all the gifts we give and get today. Yet the confidence that Christians have in Christ's resurrection, and therefore our own resurrection, liberates us to act in incredibly self-denying ways such as those Paul recounts in this epistle. Such confidence will make us increasingly like our Lord Jesus Christ in love and self-sacrifice and increasingly like him in his outlook—he endured the cross for the joy set before him. If this joy is not before your eyes, you may not endure in that to which God calls you. You may miss the greatest gift you could ever be given.

12

DECLINE

1 CORINTHIANS 16

The turn of a new year is a time for bold new initiatives, fresh starts, rethinking assumptions, and making new resolutions. But the new year is not the only time for change. Certain situations and circumstances call for new beginnings, as well. Some time ago I read an analysis revealing that the church may be faced with just such a call today: "The Bible neither describes nor promotes the local church as we know it today." Even more surprising than the actual statement is the author of it—George Barna. The statement appears in his book appropriately called *Revolution*.[1]

Barna has spent years writing almost thirty volumes on building, marketing, leading, and even turning around the local church. Yet he now perceives a problem more clearly and deeply he says than he has ever before. Barna is cautious in his phraseology, so we have to be careful not to miss the import of his last few words: "as we know it today." Barna argues that today's interconnection of Christian friendships, ministry partnerships, home Bible studies, and meetings can serve in place of the local church. He suggests that today's church ought to become more like a personalized homepage, something designed to illuminate personal interests, talents, and commitments. I guess it's not so surprising that Barna should write such a book. While he understands what he's saying to be allowed by Scripture, his arguments are clearly driven by his perceptions of polling statistics and other anecdotal evidence. In this new book Barna is simply reading the data a little differently.

Barna sums up the problem like this: "If the local church is God's answer to our spiritual needs, then why are most churches and Christians so spiritually immature and desperate?"[2] He says also, "The seven dominant spheres of influence are movies, music, television, books, the Internet, law, and family. The second tier of influencers is comprised of entities such as schools, peers, newspapers, radio, and businesses. The local church appears among entities that have little or no influence on society."[3]

As a pastor of a church and someone with a special concern for other churches, I sadly have to agree with page after page of Barna's description of some of the problems facing today's church. But when it comes to the solution, I think Scripture may give us more direction than he suggests.

What can make a difference in turning a church around? What should we do with a church that is compromised by cultural accommodation, lacks influence in the wider culture, and reflects the culture more than changes it? What do we do about local churches riven by strife, worldly-mindedness, immorality, and materialism? First Corinthians gives us Paul's answer to that very situation, and his answer does not include abandoning the church or reducing it to an optional institution. Paul uses this letter to reshape the thinking of the believers in Corinth so that they will define the church not along lines of self-expression and individual interests but along lines of humble, self-denying love and care. Here in the last chapter, Paul points to six crucial aspects of church life in need of salvage if this congregation that he loves so dearly is to continue. At the time of the letter, the Corinthian church was not far from self-destructive irrelevance.

As we study 1 Corinthians 16, we do well to think critically about our own congregations, receiving Paul's encouragement and his challenge, instruction, and direction for our lives as a united body in Christ.

Money Wisdom

As Paul concludes the letter, the first matter he addresses is what we might call *money wisdom*:

> Now about the collection for God's people: Do what I told the Galatian churches to do. On the first day of every week, each one of you should set

aside a sum of money in keeping with his income, saving it up, so that when I come no collections will have to be made. Then, when I arrive, I will give letters of introduction to the men you approve and send them with your gift to Jerusalem. If it seems advisable for me to go also, they will accompany me. (vv. 1–4)

These verses are straightforward. Paul is writing from Ephesus (in what today is the western coast of Turkey) to the church in Corinth, across the Aegean Sea in southern Greece. He had planted that church, along with many others, on what we call his second missionary journey. The Galatian churches he mentions here are those he planted in south central Turkey on his first missionary journey. At the time of his epistle to the Corinthians, there was a great famine engulfing the people in Jerusalem, and Paul encouraged churches from his missionary journeys to collect money to send to those in need.

Apparently a collection would be taken and then set aside, a collection that was to be taken on the first day of the week. Why would that day appeal to him? Perhaps because he had taught them to meet on the first day of the week. Paul had gathered the people on that particular day when he went to Troas (Acts 20:7). Additionally, John refers to the first weekday as "the Lord's day" in Revelation 1:10. This gathering time almost certainly reflects the fact that Christ's own resurrection was on the first day of the week (John 20:1), as was his first appearance to the disciples (John 20:19). We also know from early second-century sources that Christians met on the first day of the week. This regular meeting surely underlies Paul's request that the collection be taken then.

As for the collection itself, it was to be a pool of money that the Corinthians had set aside for giving. "On the first day of every week, each one of you should set aside a sum of money in keeping with his income, saving it up, so that when I come no collections will have to be made" (v. 2). The plan included sending escorts to make sure the money got to Jerusalem safely. Paul was careful with money, which is always wise. In this case, this offering is for the care of Christians elsewhere and for their physical needs. We want to encourage this kind of giving between congregations today. An important thing to note here is the nature of the caring. These were largely Gentile churches sending money to the predominantly Jewish congregations in Jerusalem. Overcoming ethnic divisions, whether Jew and Gentile or black and white, in modern-day America provides a special witness to the truth of the gospel. Frederick Buechner puts it well:

The love for equals is a human thing—of friend for friend, brother for brother. It is to love what is loving and lovely. The world smiles.

The love for the less fortunate is a beautiful thing—the love for those who suffer, for those who are poor, the sick, the failures, the unlovely. This is compassion, and it touches the heart of the world.

The love for the more fortunate is a rare thing—to love those who succeed where we fail, to rejoice without envy with those who rejoice, the love of the poor for the rich, of the black man for the white man. The world is always bewildered by its saints.

And then there is the love for the enemy—love for the one who does not love you but mocks, threatens, and inflicts pain. The tortured's love for the torturer. This is God's love. It conquers the world.[4]

A congregation demonstrates this through a wise and godly use of its money.

A Diversity of Teachers

Another crucial aspect of the Corinthians' church life in need of salvage is how they view their teachers. He writes:

After I go through Macedonia, I will come to you—for I will be going through Macedonia. Perhaps I will stay with you awhile, or even spend the winter, so that you can help me on my journey, wherever I go. I do not want to see you now and make only a passing visit; I hope to spend some time with you, if the Lord permits." (vv. 5–7)

Paul tells the Corinthians that he is planning to come to see them again after he goes through Macedonia, a place we know today as Northern Greece. That is where he planted a number of churches including those in Thessalonica and Philippi. Paul hopes to visit Corinth, and more than that, he hopes to spend some time with them. Paul is not looking for a quick trip. Having lived in Corinth for a year and a half, he would have had many friends to see, and there was clearly a lot of work to be done in the congregation.

He does not volunteer to come immediately because, he says, there is a great opportunity where he is now, in Ephesus. "But I will stay on at Ephesus until Pentecost, because a great door for effective work has opened to me, and there are many who oppose me" (vv. 8–9). Paul does not clarify exactly what this opportunity was, but we can guess that it was likely an evangelistic opportunity for the gospel in Ephesus, a time when that church was undergoing a time of special blessing and growth. We should be faithful regardless of the apparent fruit, but here is one example of Paul making a decision based in part on a consideration of the obvious effect his work was having.

Although Paul cannot come to Corinth immediately, he plans to send Timothy, his young associate. "If Timothy comes, see to it that he has nothing to fear while he is with you, for he is carrying on the work of the Lord, just as I am. No one, then, should refuse to accept him. Send him on his way in peace so that he may return to me. I am expecting him along with the brothers" (vv. 10–11). Paul knew that the Corinthians would rather have him than Timothy, but he exhorts them to provide for this teacher, who, in God's sovereignty, is available to come right then.

Perhaps whom they really wanted was Apollos. "Now about our brother Apollos: I strongly urged him to go to you with the brothers. He was quite unwilling to go now, but he will go when he has the opportunity" (v. 12). Perhaps Apollos was grieved over his divisive and worldly "fans" in the Corinthian congregation and therefore wanted to stay away until the fuss had died down. As we look at these various teachers, we are reminded that we must trust God's providence for his timings in giving a congregation a particular teacher. Hard-bitten or soft, young or old, eloquent or tongue-tied—whatever their strengths and weaknesses, we should love them for their careful teaching of the one gospel.

A Clear Commitment

A third matter Paul addresses here at the end of the epistle is the need for a clear commitment.

"Be on your guard," he writes, "stand firm in the faith; be men of courage; be strong. Do everything in love" (vv. 13–14). I am not sure why Paul interrupts his personal remarks here; perhaps his comments about his delay in returning to Corinth and sending Timothy instead and perhaps his remarks about Apollos have reminded him afresh of the struggles the church has been having. So Paul exhorts the Corinthian believers to develop a military self-discipline—"Be on your guard; stand firm in the faith; be men of courage; be strong"—combined with love — "Do everything in love."

Verses 13 and 14 may not seem to go together naturally, but upon reflection we see that they do. The Corinthian congregation was under attack. People were teaching false doctrines; they were disparaging marriage and even denying the resurrection; they were dividing into factions. In the midst of all this, what they needed was to be alert and firm; they needed courage and strength to persevere. Following Christ was clearly difficult for them.

Paul's words serve as a warning to us. Sometimes in our marketing zeal we present the Christian life to unbelievers as one long, unbroken stroll in the park with our heavenly friend. It is no such thing. Every true Christian knows joys—yes, tremendous joys—but in this world, those joys are in the context of trial and temptation, of difficulty and struggle. Being a Christian is certainly worth whatever struggle may come with it, but we all must stop and count the cost before setting out to follow Christ. We need all the courage and strength we can get for what lies ahead of us, yet the strength that we as Christians are called to have is not one of contracted, constricted, tough, tense, coldness. Rather, it is an expansive strength, one that is outgoing, kind, caring, and warm. Do everything in love, as Paul exhorts these people in the midst of a serious spiritual war.

If you think that this is foolish counsel, the spiritual equivalent of the peacenik in wartime sticking flowers down the barrel of the soldiers' rifles, then you have not understood very well the kind of love that we are talking about. Christian love is no mere abstract theory; it is not a disembodied, unengaged cheerfulness, like some drug-induced state. Christian love calls us not to desert but to stand guard, not to give up but to stand firm, not to avoid conflict in cowardice but to defend truth in courage. In short, the Christian understanding of love calls not for a yielding weakness but for a persevering strength. One cannot long be misunderstood for the other.

If this is still unclear to you, consider the apostles. Consider Paul. Do you not see strength and courage and firmness and a careful alertness in his words to the Corinthians, in his persevering through wild beasts in Ephesus, and all the other difficulties he faced as he preached the gospel? Most of all, consider the love of Christ, who is the essence of love. My friends, what is the supreme evidence of Christ's love for us? It is his giving of himself to die on the cross. What motivated God to give his only Son? His love (see John 3:16). What motivated the Lord Jesus to lay down his life? It was love. Jesus taught, "Greater love has no one than this, that he lay down his life for his friends" (John 15:13). Can you imagine Christ going to the cross while lacking these characteristics? Pray that you as a Christian and we as a body would model this kind of strong love. We need this combination, this clear commitment of loving strength, that we see here in Paul's letter.

Good Examples

The fourth matter Paul brings up again here is the importance of good examples:

> You know that the household of Stephanas were the first converts in Achaia, and they have devoted [addicted] themselves to the service of the saints. I urge you, brothers, to submit to such as those and to everyone who joins in the work, and labors at it. I was glad when Stephanas, Fortunatus and Achaicus arrived, because they have supplied what was lacking from you. For they refreshed my spirit and yours also. Such men deserve recognition. (vv. 15–18)

Achaia was the area of Greece in which Corinth was situated. Stephanas was mentioned in 1 Corinthians 1 as having been baptized by Paul himself, evidently a fairly unusual thing. It seems that Stephanas was the Corinthian charged by the congregation in Corinth to bring a letter to Paul in Ephesus, asking about the various matters that Paul has addressed in this letter and informing him about the other situations he addresses in the epistle. Stephanas is accompanied here by two men, Fortunatus and Achaicus, whom scholars suggest were either slaves or freed slaves. Their names mean "Lucky" and "the guy from Achaia," respectively. Paul mentions all three of these men as having done good work through refreshing his spirit and encouraging him.

Paul describes Stephanas and his household as those who "devoted themselves to the service of the saints." They gave themselves to serving God's people. I love the way the King James Version renders this: "They have *addicted* themselves to the service of the saints." Brothers and sisters, we want to see congregations that are besotted with serving and preferring one another. We want people to care for those members who are away from their church home—in the military, or in seminary, or on a missions trip, or at college, or in retirement homes. We want people to give themselves in serving at weddings and other special services, in caring for the physical needs of older saints, in delighting to give money to help poorer members with expenses, in being willing to walk through a difficult time with younger Christians, in giving time to holding someone accountable, and in providing transportation. We want to be typified by a cheerful giving of our time to others, to be known for inconveniencing ourselves with great regularity for God's people.

Something in this last chapter compels our attention. Paul writes, "I urge you, brothers, to submit to such as these and to everyone who joins in the work, and labors at it" (vv. 15b–16). Paul calls on the other Christians in Corinth to submit to servants like Stephanas and the others who join in his work. Paul does not mean that whoever sweeps the floor of the sanctuary should be the pastor, but it *does* mean that those who are leading the way should be obeyed. Paul is also not suggesting submission to the sort of self-important, do-nothing teachers that had clearly troubled the Corinthian congregation. No, Paul here encourages the Corinthian church—and our churches today—to notice those who refresh the saints and who labor for their good and to respect them. In fact, he says, recognize them, honor them, and celebrate them. Take them as your pattern, your guides, your examples. We must pray that God will help us to do that in our congregations. Try to notice who is serving. Honor them, thank them, pray for them. Gossip positively about them. Follow their example.

A Larger Vision

A fifth matter that Paul raises with this troubled congregation is their need for a larger vision:

> The churches in the province of Asia send you greetings. Aquila and Priscilla greet you warmly in the Lord, and so does the church that meets at their house. All the brothers here send you greetings. Greet one another with a holy kiss. I, Paul, write this greeting in my own hand. (vv. 19–21)

There are lots of greetings here, which was a common part of ancient letters. The format is not all that different from how we end our letters today. But even here in these greetings Paul is teaching.

First, he sets forth Aquila and Priscilla as more good examples for the Corinthians to emulate. Aquila and Priscilla had lived in Corinth when Paul was there. They were known to the Corinthian Christians. They have become models by their service of hosting the church. As leatherworkers or tentmakers, they may have had a very large, enclosed yard or an open area where they worked—dried, stretched out leather, and sewed tents. It would have been a natural place for a large group of people to gather. Churches didn't have buildings dedicated for fellowship and worship until a few hundred years after Christ. Someone had to go to the trouble of hosting the congregation in Ephesus. Aquila and Priscilla were willing to do that.

Second, Paul challenges the Corinthian believers to live up to their profession, even by the call to "greet one another with a holy kiss." He says the same thing at the end of other letters: when he writes again to the Corinthians, and to the Thessalonians and the Romans. Peter says it too at the end of his first epistle. But it would have had special punch at the end of this letter. The point here is not the kiss, which is a culturally conditioned greeting. In some places around the globe, kisses serve as greetings; in other places they do not, and it is generally a good idea to know the difference! But the significant thing for us here is that Paul is urging this division-ridden congregation to greet each other, and to do so with love, propriety, and sincere affection. He has called on them to surpass one another in building up the saints, in doing everything for the edification of the church. This letter has been a call to unity—a unity of the church that is to reflect God's own unity. Now here, even at the end, Paul turns common customs to pedagogical purpose.

Third, Paul calls them on to this larger vision of love and care that stretches between congregations. We see it in the call to take up a collection to help with the needs of the Christians in Jerusalem. We see it in the greetings he sends from the congregations around Ephesus. Paul is subtly building up their understanding that they are vitally connected to a larger movement, a larger family.

Friends, I don't know about you, but I am encouraged when I consider what God is doing elsewhere. I think we are helped toward better, more godly, more Christlike congregations if we know something about what God is doing in other churches. We are a part of something much larger than our local congregation. Other congregations are not teams we compete with; they are families of treasured brothers and sisters that we want to love and serve and encourage and pray for. They are full of sheep for whom Christ died. We are helped to follow him better by remembering that and expressing it in our speech and our prayers. We want an ever-growing vision of God's ever-growing kingdom.

Grace and Love

Finally, Paul speaks to them at the very end of this remarkable letter about grace and love. "If anyone does not love the Lord—a curse be on him. Come, O Lord! The grace of the Lord Jesus be with you. My love to all of you in Christ Jesus. Amen" (vv. 22–24). It becomes clear here that in Christianity there is no middle ground of religious neutrality—"If anyone does not love the Lord—a curse be on him." There is no middle ground; it is either love Christ or be cursed by him.

God has made us and deserves all of us—our wholehearted affection and complete obedience.

We have, however, disobeyed him and not loved him. In fact, Christ's crucifixion is a summary statement of the entire world's response to God. The most amazing gift ever given, returned to sender, with a rejection inspired by spite, even hatred. This is the situation we have all been in and in which unbelievers remain today. God is a great sovereign who accepts only submission. Anything else is opposition to him.

We see our failures within the church, and unbelievers see them too. Nevertheless, the call remains, and we can go forward because of Paul's final words: "The grace of the Lord Jesus be with you." Grace is favor given that we have not merited; grace is given despite us. We have actually merited disfavor.

What is the grace of the Lord Jesus? It is the grace of God available to us in our sins through Christ. Christ came and lived a perfect life. Christ in no way lived a life of hatred to God, nor of disobedience to his will. He obeyed perfectly. He died on the cross as part of his loving, voluntary identification with us, and by his death he accepted God's wrath as a substitute for everyone who would ever repent of their sins and trust in him. God's grace is extended to sinners through Christ.

Do you know this grace? If not, why not begin now with a new life? Ask God to forgive you of your sins for Christ's sake and to fill you with his Spirit. Live for God in obedience to him; live with him now self-consciously as your Lord, and the change will be remarkable. Paul called it a new creation; Jesus called it a new birth. Friends, this is far more important than a pay raise, losing a few pounds, or finding that new job.

My Christian brothers and sisters, are you showing such Christlike love and grace to others? Wife, are you loving your husband? Husband, are you caring for your wife as you should? Friend, have you reached out to those who are away from home? Son, have you expressed your thanks to your parents? How about you who have been sinned against? What have you done to express honest forgiveness and to further honest reconciliation? Brother or sister, how have you cared for other members who, like these Corinthians here, seem trapped in their sins? Have you given time to seeing them, spending time with them, praying for them, asking them tough questions, encouraging them, exhorting them, loving them?

I wonder how we as a church think we are ever going to be very good at evangelism or world missions if we are not very good at applying the gospel of Christ to our own hearts and to the relationships we have right in our own churches. It is my prayer that we will see more and more evidences of God's love and grace in our congregations.

Conclusion

Paul ends his letter with these words: "My love to all of you in Christ Jesus" (v. 24). We began our study by considering Paul's kind comments to the Corinthians in the opening of the epistle. We marveled at the fact that in this letter to a famously messed-up church, Paul began with a sincere identification of God's gracious work in them. Now we have come to the end of a letter that has been pretty rough at points—Paul's outcry against their foolish, worldly-minded divisions, their astounding tolerance of immorality, their gospel-denying litigiousness, their confusion over marriage, their selfishness, and their resurrection-denying heresy—and what does Paul say in closing? "My love to all of you in Christ Jesus."

Oh, my friends, if you are ever going to be used as a guide and friend, a change agent or evangelist, a discipler or a refresher of spirits like Stephanas, you must love. Henry Drummond frequently gave a now-famous lecture on 1 Corinthians 13, and at one point in it, when considering the guilelessness and sincerity in the vision of love presented in that marvelous chapter, he said, "You will find, if you think for a moment, that the people who influence you are people who believe in you. In an atmosphere of suspicion men shrivel up; but in that atmosphere they expand, and find encouragement and educative fellowship."[5]

Instruction that comes through yelling and scolding seldom instructs very much. Those so approached naturally feel defensive. For most of us, our humility is too little and our pride too great to learn very much from people who do not love us. But let people know that you love them in words and deeds, let them know that you are on their side, let them know that your interest is their good, and you will have a much readier audience and a much more responsive student.

That is what Paul was praying for and working toward with this congregation in Corinth. He had labored over it, but at the time of his letter, it had become unhinged and almost lost. Paul could have responded in anger over the years he wasted there, the prayers expended to no purpose, and the teaching ignored.

Instead, by God's grace, surely knowing his own need for God's grace, Paul communicated to the Corinthians in love and tender concern. He instructed them clearly in this letter, sometimes even sharply, but never without love. Paul knew that God's Spirit was at work in this congregation, however unlikely a claim that might have seemed from time to time. From their divisions the Spirit was creating a unity to reflect his own within the Trinity. From their natural carnality and sin the Spirit was remaking them to be a people marked by a holiness that would reflect his holiness. And from their busy, narrow self-interestedness the Spirit was breaking their hearts with the gospel of Jesus Christ and fashioning them into a people of love to reflect his love.

If you pray for God to do this with us and in our midst, in your heart and mine, in my congregation and yours, then join me in affirming it by saying together now this final word in 1 Corinthians—"Amen."

Appendix

QUESTIONS ABOUT 1 CORINTHIANS 7

1) **In 1 Corinthians 7:1 is Paul teaching that it is good for a man not to touch a woman, or is that a Corinthian teaching that Paul is commenting on?** The whole chapter makes sense if you take this as a distorted teaching that Paul is responding to. The wrong teaching was that men were not to "touch a woman," a euphemism for sexual intimacy, which essentially brought into question the entire institution of marriage.

2) **Is singleness better than marriage (7:1, 8, 35, 38, 40)?** For some people it is better. But the normal creation ordinance is marriage (Gen. 1:28; 2:18). Paul says here (7:2) that "every man should have his own wife, and each woman her own husband." Marriage is the norm. Not until Cyprian in the third century was there an exaltation of virginity as a superior calling. Even then it was minimal and did not become a widespread notion until Ambrose in the fourth century.

3) **Does Paul think sex is bad (7:6)?** No; sex is simply part of what married people experience that can make devotion to God more complicated. The "concession" that Paul mentions in this passage is not sexual relations but the temporary abstinence from them, which was, perhaps, what the ascetics at Corinth were teaching and practicing.

4) **Are Paul's words in 1 Corinthians 7:10, 12, 25, and 40 inspired?** They are. Paul understands his instructions in verse 10 to approximate Christ's

prohibition of divorce. In verse 12 he is simply continuing to teach, without referencing any particular teaching of Jesus'. This is what he means again in verse 25. And in verse 40 Paul is asserting his dependability not over against Jesus but over against the false teachers mentioned in the first four chapters of the letter. Notice the care to preserve the words of Jesus that is assumed here. Paul resisted any temptation to invent such words, regardless of how convenient it would have been to do so.

5) Is divorce allowed (7:10–16)? Yes, in the case of desertion that has already broken a marriage. Jesus' teaching is found in Matthew 5:31–32; 19:3–9; Mark 10:2–12; and Luke 16:18. But basically the answer is no for all kinds of reasons. Marriage is important because it is a reflection of Christ's love for his people (cf. Mal. 2:4–6; Matt. 19:6; Mark 10:9). With the exception of a very few specific situations, we have no more right to dissolve our marriage than we do to take our own lives. In marriage it is God that joins us to our spouse.

6) Is remarriage okay (7:11, 15, 39)? It is not all right to marry anyone who has wrongly left his or her spouse (v. 11). Matthew 5:32 and Luke 16:18 seem to disallow remarriage. But here in 1 Corinthians 7 remarriage seems to be allowed for the person deserted (v. 15) or a widow, provided she marrys a Christian (v. 39). When divorce is permitted, remarriage is assumed.

7) Are "holy" children to be baptized as infants (7:14)? No, this passage does not suggest that infants should be baptized. This simply means that they are not illegitimate.

8) What does Paul mean by "become uncircumcised" (7:18)? He means that a Christian is not to make a point of acting like a non-Jew; perhaps undergoing surgery to try to make one appear less circumcised.

9) Is slavery okay (7:20–24)? No; and verse 21 suggests that slaves ought to get free if the opportunity arises. Verse 23 forbids putting oneself voluntarily into slavery, something that people might have considered for economic reasons. But challenging slavery in the general social, economic, and political structures of the Roman Empire was not the Christian's immediate goal or duty. One can live as a Christian slave (see Eph. 6:5–8; Col. 3:23; 1 Tim. 6:1–2).

10) What is "the present crisis" (7:26)? The present crisis Paul mentions is either (1) the life's situation in which Christians find themselves between the resurrection and Christ's return, or (2) the increasing tribulation traditionally expected at the end of the age (Luke 21:23), which Paul assumed was already occurring at the time of his writing, or (3) an immediate limited situation of some kind, perhaps a natural disaster such as famine. There are archaeological and literary evidences of this. There are also records of earth-quakes, and if we consider this along with Matthew 24:7, 9 and Mark 13:17, you can see why Paul would give this advice. Other immediate situations in Paul's day might have included political instability or religious persecution. Finally, (4), "the present crisis" might simply be referring to the ideal of living with the end in view.

11) What is the "short" time to which Paul refers (7:29)? Paul is referring either to the comparative brevity of the individual's life (James 4:14; 1 Pet. 1:24) or to the immanence of Christ's return (cf. Luke 14:26; Rom. 13:11–12; 1 Cor. 1:7–8). The future has become clear to us, and that affects how we live.

12) What does it mean for the married to act as if they're not married (7:29)? Paul means that Christians are not to make their spouse their ultimate priority. Marriage, along with everything else in life, must be kept under an eternal perspective.

13) Does 1 Corinthians 7:29–35 teach asceticism? No; it teaches moderation and a heavenly perspective on this world. In 7:3 Paul specifically enjoined sexual relations as a duty between a husband and his wife. The uncertainty of the world should take from our hearts the love of it. Heavenly matters are never to be secondary. Any preference Paul has for singleness is not rooted in a desire to deny pleasure but rather to encourage God-centeredness.

NOTES

Chapter 1: "Forgetfulness"

1. *Relevant*, May/June 2005.

2. William Gouge, in James Reid, *Memoirs of the Westminster Divines* (Edinburgh: Banner of Truth, 1983), 357.

3. Ibid.

4. Ibid., 358.

5. Richard Sibbes, "The Rich Poverty," *Works of Richard Sibbes* (Edinburgh: Banner of Truth, 1983), 6:254.

6. David Prior, *The Message of 1 Corinthians* (Downers Grove, IL: InterVarsity, 1985), 22.

Chapter 2: "Division"

1. A. W. Tozer, in *Worship by the Book*, ed. Don Carson (Grand Rapids, MI: Zondervan, 2002), 151.

2. Jonathan Edwards, "The Nakedness of Job," *The Works of Jonathan Edwards*, 10:404, 410.

Chapter 4: "Sin"

1. David Brooks, "War and Men at Yale," *The Daily Standard*, October 29, 2001.

2. Marsha Witten, *All Is Forgiven: The Secular Message in American Protestantism* (Princeton, NJ: Princeton University Press, 1993), 111.

3. Sally Quinn, *The Washington Post*, July 12, 1999, C2.

4. Charles Spurgeon, *Morning and Evening*, ed. Alistair Begg (Wheaton, IL: Crossway, 2003), October 15, evening.

5. Bruce Winter, "1 Corinthians," in *New Bible Commentary, 21st Century Edition*, ed. Gordon Wenham, J. A. Motyer, D. A. Carson, and R. T. France (Downers Grove, IL: InterVarsity, 1994), 1169.

6. William Arnot, *Studies in Proverbs: Laws from Heaven for Life on Earth*, 5th ed. (Grandville, MI: Kregel Classics, 1978), 578–80.

Chapter 5: "Asceticism"

1. Bruce Winter, "1 Corinthians," in *New Bible Commentary, 21st Century Edition*, ed. Gordon Wenham, J. A. Motyer, D. A. Carson, and R. T. France (Downers Grove, IL: InterVarsity, 1994), 1173.

2. Richard Sibbes, "The Spiritual Man's Aim," *Works of Richard Sibbes* (Edinburgh: Banner of Truth, 1983), 4:39–58.

3. Recounted in Philip Yancey, *Soul Survivor: How My Faith Survived the Church* (London: Hodder & Stoughton, 2003), 81.

Chapter 6: "Disobedience"

1. Samuel Jones, "Treatise of Church Discipline," in *Polity*, ed. Mark Dever (Washington DC, 2001), 143.

2. D. A. Carson, *For the Love of God*, vol. 1 (Wheaton, IL: Crossway, 1998), May 25 entry.

Chapter 7: "Legalism"

1. Charles Spurgeon, in a sermon on Psalm 112:7.

2. Edward D. Pollard, Daniel Gurden Stevens, *Luther Rice: Pioneer in Missions and Education* (Columbia, SC: Watafind Books, 1995), 91.

3. Ibid.

Chapter 8: "Autonomy"

1. Dio Chyrsostom.

2. G. K. Chesterton, *Orthodoxy* (San Francisco: Ignatius Press, 1995), 31–32.

3. Wayne Grudem, *Systematic Theology: An Introduction to Biblical Doctrine* (Grand Rapids, MI: Zondervan, 1995), 458–59.

Chapter 9: "Thoughtlessness"

1. Mark Noll, *A History of Christianity in the United States and Canada* (Grand Rapids, MI: Eerdmans, 1992), 141.

2. John Bunyan, "Grace Abounding," in *Famous Conversions*, ed. Hugh Kerr and John Mulder (Grand Rapids, MI: Eerdmans, 1994), 50.

Chapter 10: "Selfishness"

1. Cited by Richard Shenkman, *Legends, Lies & Cherished Myths of American History* (New York: Harper Paperbacks, 1994), 40.

2. John Winterson Richards, *Xenophobe's Guide to the Welsh* (Opal Books, 1999), 31.

3. Jonathan Edwards, *Charity and Its Fruit* (Edinburgh: Banner of Truth, 1969), 327–28.

4. Ibid., 330.

5. Ibid., 332.

6. Ibid., 346.

Chapter 11: "Death"

1. Dave Shiflett, *Exodus: Why Americans Are Fleeing Liberal Churches for Conservative Christianity* (New York: Sentinel, 2005), 15–16.
2. Thais.
3. Lee Strobel, *The Case for Christ: A Journalist's Personal Investigation of the Evidence for Jesus* (Grand Rapids, MI: Zondervan, 1998).
4. Garry Wills, *Certain Trumpets: The Nature of Leadership* (New York: Simon & Schuster, 1995), 42–43.

Chapter 12: "Decline"

1. George Barna, *Revolution* (Ventura, CA: Barna Books, 2005), 37.
2. Ibid., 30.
3. Ibid., 118.
4. Frederick Buechner, *The Magnificent Defeat* (New York: HarperOne, 1985), 105.
5. Henry Drummond, *The Greatest Thing in the World* (Grand Rapids, MI: Revell, 1981).

Scripture Index